THE TAO OF SEX

素 女 玄 道

THE TAO OF SEX

The Essence of Medical Prescriptions (Ishimpō)

Howard S. Levy and Akira Ishihara

Richard Stodart (Illustrator)

Integral Publishing
Lower Lake, California

First published by Shibundo Publishers, Japan, 1968
Second revised edition, 1969
First paperback edition published by Harper & Row, 1970
Third revised edition, 1989

Printed in the United States

Integral Publishing
P.O. Box 1030
Lower Lake, CA 95457

Cover art and inside illustrations by Richard Stodart, San Francisco

Cover photography by George Ward, San Anselmo, California

To the memory of R. H. van Gulik,
the great sinologist and innovator
who first made available to the West
the lore of ancient Chinese sexology.

Library of Congress Catalog Card Number: 89-08346
ISBN 0-94125-43-3 (cloth)
ISBN 0-94125-44-1 (paper)

93 92 91 90
10 9 8 7 6 5 4 3

Contents

Preface to the Third Revised Edition

The Taoists of ancient China looked upon sex as a vehicle for enlightenment, providing that the sexual urge was properly harnessed. To them, sex and spirituality were interdependent.

In the tenth century, a Japanese physician compiled a bedroom monograph for Japanese sovereigns, showing them how to regulate their sex lives harmoniously in a polygamous environment. He based his advocacies on the age-old writings of Taoism. These Taoist texts are a tribute to ancient Chinese savants who wrote detailed treatises on sexology long before the world knew the term.

The texts presented in this volume are primarily male-oriented but the fifth chapter tells women how to invigorate the female element and likewise recapture the bloom of youth. The Way is open to both sexes and it has a unisex purpose, namely to transform the boudoir into an altar for body-mind enlightenment through meditative enrichment and spiritual transmutation of the sex urge. We are told not to regard sex as a mere physical function but rather as a catalyst for vibrant health and enriched being.

The techniques described in this book were part and parcel of ancient religious practices designed to redirect sexual energies into spiritual channels, with such side benefits as health enhancement and rejuvenation.

This is a new edition of a classic Taoist treatise inaccessible to the general public for many years. The translation combines readability with accuracy and is also clearly explained.

Since the 1970s, the sexual orientations of Eastern Taoist and Tantric practices have intrigued a growing number of Westerners. Some have derived the practical benefits of enhanced health, a harmonious outlook, and a kinder, gentler way to view sexual pleasures. The present work, originally conceived more than two decades ago, assumes greater relevance with the passing years.

Howard S. Levy, Ph.D.
Yokohama, Japan

Disclaimer

No statement in this book should be construed as sexological or medical advice to the reader by the authors or the publisher.   It is recommended that those wishing to practice Taoist sexuality should find a qualified teacher, and those having sexual questions or medical problems should consult a qualified physician.

Our Techniques of Collaboration

While residing in Japan early in 1968, my attention was drawn to a Japanese translation of the sexological portion of an ancient Heian text called *Ishimpō* 医心方. As I examined the book, I became aware that the principal scholarly contribution towards its compilation had been that of Dr. Akira Ishihara, who had made the Japanese translation and also furnished a detailed series of annotations to the text and a bibliographical essay. Dr. Ishihara and I both happened to be living in Yokohama, and in February, 1968 I proposed to him that we collaborate on the preparation of an English translation of the twenty-eighth section of *Ishimpō*. He assented with enthusiasm. We completed the present study in early October, 1968, about eight months after we had started it.

Using Dr. Ishihara's work as my guide, I prepared an English translation of the text, examining both the original Chinese and Dr. Ishihara's Japanese translation. We held periodic meetings, during which he checked the translation and offered critical comments. The same procedure was followed for the footnotes and the introductions to the chapters—for this information I leaned heavily on Dr. Ishihara's published researches. Dr. Ishihara further prepared several of the important footnotes in Japanese, from which I then made my translations. I readied the indices of sex and medical terms, resorting to Dr. Ishihara's findings for my translations. In his triple capacity as a Japanese physician, practitioner of Chinese medicine, and an expert on the ancient Taoist texts, Dr. Ishihara's insights and understanding were the essential elements which facilitated our collaborative efforts—my contribution consisted mainly of transmitting his knowledge into English. For the annotated bibliography, I prepared the essay, all of the Chinese and most of the Japanese items. Dr. Ishihara made available to me the last four issures of *Kaishaku to kanshō*, which provided us with invaluable

1

bibliographical information.   The index was prepared jointly.   For the appendices, I wrote the first one on the history of Chinese medicine in Japan by relying exclusively on Dr. Ishihara's published writings. The second and third appendices, relating to Chinese medicine and acupuncture, were made in the following way.   We developed impromptu dialogues and made tape recordings of these dialogues.   Dr. Ishihara transcribed them into Japanese, after which I added the English translations.   The purpose of this technique was to elicit detailed responses from the expert (Ishihara) through questions posed by the Western novice (Levy).   In conclusion, I hope that our techniques of collaboration, as explained above, may suggest fruitful joint research techniques to other Japanese and Western scholars.

Howard S. Levy
October 10, 1968
Yokohama, Japan

Introductory Remarks

Taoism refers to an ancient philosophy that arose in China more than two thousand years ago, during the latter half of the Chou dynasty. The Taoists advocated that life be lived in harmony with nature, and they venerated woman because they believed that she was closer than man to nature's primordial forces. Some among them thought that woman was to be treasured because her body contained the elements indispensable for attaining to physical male immortality. They wrote many treatises about woman, sex, and the Tao; as the texts we have translated will show, they regarded the Tao of Sex not as an end in itself but as a means to enrich the body and enlighten the spirit. The Taoists advocated widespread sexual indulgence without emission. A battle of the sexes was depicted in which each partner tried to keep his or her own fluid while getting the vital fluid of the other. Taiost sexologists took a dim view of romantic love and asserted that monogamy was mutually injurious. The man was avised to make every effort to form unions with a number of young unmarried women under thirty and to avoid sex with ladies who were either thirty or older or had borne children. Many of these thoughts circulated in China two thousand years ago, during the Han dynasty. The famed Han historian Ssu-ma Ch'ien claimed in his *Historical Records* that a revered religious and medical sage of remote antiquity known as the Yellow Emperor had retained his semen while having intercourse with twelve hundred women.[1]

---

1. Ssu-ma Ch'ien made this notation at the end of a brief biography of the Yellow Emperor. He explained how the Yellow Emperor came to power, ascribed to him the initiation of palace regulations on palace utensils, dress, and currency, and concluded with these words: "He was on the throne one hundred years; he controlled 1,200 women and in broad daylight ascended as an Immortal."

3

Since the Yellow Emperor was a Heavenly Immortal and a paragon of perfection, the Taoists argued that emulation of his sex behavior was tantamount to securing a one-way ticket to Paradise. "To go to Heaven in broad daylight as he did, have intercourse without emission as he did," they seemed to advise.

These advocates of a " in Many we trust " theory disavowed passionate attachment to one woman and directed the man to maximize contacts and minimize emissions. The texts we have translated include a large number of Chinese sources which date from about the first to the eighth century; these were assembled in Japan and printed in the tenth century. The sources vary in content, but they all look at sex in about the same way. Again and again they assert that the fulfillment of sexual needs is through emotional self-control and manipulation of the partner. The man is to keep his cool while agitating the woman so that she loses hers. Almost every chapter in this monograph on the bedroom arts serves as a kind of sex education manual on what every man should know. He is advised repeatedly that health and longevity are achieved by being sexually promiscuous while hoarding the semen treasure. It is essential, he is told, to change partners frequently. Prolonged intercourse with one woman benefits the male increasingly less, because monogamy is said to have an adverse effect on the quality of the woman's emissions. The best bed partner is a virgin, the best age is between fourteen and nineteen, and the best intercourse is with three, nine, or eleven women nightly. These odd numbers were considered male, part of an ancient *yin-yang* cosmology that explained everything in the world as a union of female and male elements. According to this theory, Heaven was male, Earth female, and man a reflection of the endless energies of both. Old men, presumably affluent, were told that if they carried out to the letter the instructions quoted in our text to change partners frequently, they could thereby increase virility beyond measure and recapture the sexual prowess of youth.

Our monograph on the bedroom arts has rightly been called a bible of sex. There is a kind of religious fervor about the writing; the Word is never questioned, and through sex the faithful are exhorted to seek salvation. Male readers are cautioned to maintain self-control at all times and to avoid emotional extremes. A man must never enter the boudoir depressed or overjoyed, but rather approach the inner recesses with mental composure and philosophic calm. To gain the Kingdom he stays aloof as he manipulates the woman, getting her to emit in order to enhance his physiological well-being. During coitus he has to retain his semen, for to lose it is to lose his Taoist soul. If he finds himself on the verge of abandoning self-control, biblical authorities caution him to break off the union and change partners. In that way, he breaks the spell that leads to emission and to failure of the Quest. The Taoists believed that the way to attain and keep physiological well-being was through proper application of the bedroom arts. Acting on this hypothesis, in the first millenium of the Western era they set forth the Tao of Sex for all to follow. This Tao is preserved in the monograph we have chosen for translation, the only one in China or Japan replete with extensive passages from sexology texts lost for many centruries and unobtainable elsewhere. The tenth-century compiler of the monograph further succeeded in weaving passages together so as to form coherent and persuasive essays.

The Taoist adepts of ancient China revered the Yellow Emperor and adopted what they believed to be his medical theories. Many of them became physicians, and in this curative capacity they were received by emperors and aristocratic courtiers as honored guests. They gave instructions in boudoir practices to men who were surfeited with female companions; this was especially true of the T'ang (seventh to tenth century), which was characterized by vast numbers of prostitutes, female entertainers, and concubines.[2] In a practical way, therefore, the sex handbooks of the Taoists served as first-aid kits for the Chinese gentleman of leisure, whose well-being was threatened by unending amorous play and unrepressed profligation. The Emperor had thousands of women in his harem, and he was on intimate terms with at least several dozen. To him, advice on how to conserve was advice on

---

2. See essay by H. S. Levy on T'ang prostitution called " T'ang Women of Pleasure " (*Sinologica*, VIII, 2, 1965, 89–114). He describes how prostitutes and entertainers served a wide range of social classes, from the imperial family to the troops. The T'ang being an age of poetry, when a kept woman and a high official were forced to part, the moment was often recorded in verse. (Cf. H. S. Levy, translation of the T'ang monograph *Pen-shih shih* 本事詩 in *Sinologica*, X, 1, 1968, called " The Original Incidents of Poems," 7–22.)

how to survive. The Emperor who guarded against leakage in nightly intercourse may have become neurotic, but he was saved from over-addiction to aphrodisiacs and utter collapse. The texts before us reflect a polygamous Chinese society in which women were easily available to the ruling class; otherwise, the instructions on maximizing contacts and changing partners would have been impractical and unrealistic.

Our manual occupies a special place in traditional Chinese writings, for it is written in a factual style and it stresses physiological, rather than psychological, states of being. It is the antithesis of the Confucian gentleman-type essay, in which an anonymous author will refer obliquely to a woman's charms but piously avoid reference to anatomical details and to the movements within the bedcovers. Our *Tao of Sex* guide reverses the process. It makes no effort to titillate the reader or to appeal to prurient interest but, instead, sets forth in plain words the most beneficial ways to have intercourse, the ways to prepare for it, the things to do, and the things to avoid. The bedroom manual includes chapters on how to use aphrodisiacs, how to enlarge the overly small penis, how to shrink the overly large vagina, and how to lessen the pain from coitus suffered by a virgin or an older woman. It also sets forth the proper positions of intercourse to be practiced and prescribes sex to cure debilitation from over-indulgence in sex. These chapters are written in matter-of-fact prose, without embellishment. The major problem for the translator is with words rather than phrases, for the texts abound in terms of special sexual significance not to be found in the lexicons. Dr. Akira Ishihara, who has devoted years of study to these problems, has made a major contribution to scholarship through his renderings of such terms. His contributions are reflected throughout our joint translation and annotation; he has further noted the rare passage in the monograph that may have been miscopied or transmitted incorrectly.

The text reads in places like an anatomy handbook, as much of it is based on scientific observation. There are also comments on folk customs and taboos that reflect the superstitions of an earlier age. These provide valuable information for the folklorist, since they are from primary sources. The apostles in our bible of sex include sage-immortals of antiquity such as the Yellow Emperor and the Queen Mother of the West; women in the forefront of Taoist sex reform such as the

Woman Plain, the Woman Selective, and the Woman Profound; and an assortment of male Taoist Immortals. However, the reader is well advised to ignore the medium and concentrate on the message. The texts from which the citations are taken are no longer extant, there is no angel's adversary, and all questions are answered within a Taoist sexological framework of Han, Sui, or T'ang times. We have made every effort to be accurate in our translations and to convey the spirit as well as the letter of the texts, but some of the statements in the original sources are cryptic, and others may be based on erroneous transmissions. There are also some philological problems which are extremely difficult to unravel and resolve. The Chinese text, collated by Dr. Ishihara, is available in a separate booklet. Interested and qualified readers are invited to check our translations, correct our errors, and suggest ways and means to make further improvements on what we have done. There are many metaphors in the text for terms of sexual significance, such as *jade gate* for *vagina* and *jade stalk* for *penis*; our translation technique has been to retain the metaphor in the English rendition and provide the modern equivalent in a footnote and in an index of sex terms. The same technique is followed for medical terms. Considerable supplementary information has been provided on Chinese medical practice and on the use of aphrodisiacs, and essential textual annotations have been added. We have also made available an annotated bibliography on Sino-Japanese sexology, in order to assist the specialist who wishes to examine in greater depth questions touched upon in the course of our study.

Akira Ishihara
Howard S. Levy
October 10, 1968
Yokohama, Japan

History of the Text

The text which we have selected for translation is one of thirty detailed sections of a voluminous medical treatise called *The Essence of Medical Prescriptions (Ishimpō)*.[3] These sections were grouped by topic by Tamba Yasuyori, a Chinese physician living in Japan in the late tenth century. Mr. Tamba was of distinguished lineage, tracing his ancestry to a late Han dynasty emperor. He started the treatise in 982 and completed it in 984. It became a standard reference work for Japanese medical practitioners, and today it is the oldest monograph on medicine extant in Japan. It is an extremely valuable repository of ancient Chinese works, citing more than two hundred Han, Sui, and T'ang sources, most of which are not available elsewhere. These Chinese sources partially survive, therefore, through its citations. Soon after completion, *The Essence of Medical Prescriptions* came to be widely used in and around the palace as the best work of its kind. Tamba's descendants revered it and wrote supplementary studies for more than a century after his death, but by the Kamakura era (thirteenth-fourteenth centuries), Japanese physicians had transferred their interests to medical studies adopted from Sung China. Tamba's work was consequently consulted less and less, but while ignored it remained secure within

---

3. For a detailed discussion of the publication of this text and its subsequent history, see Dr. Ishihara's bibliographical essay in *Ishimpō* 医心方, especially pp. 246–63. *Ishimpō* was published by Shibundō 至文堂, Tokyo, on November 15, 1967, and the first edition was sold out in about six months. As of now (October, 1968), a second edition has not been published. Dr. Ishihara was joined in this publication effort by illustrator Takada Shōjirō 高田正二郎, who has also illustrated our book; editor Mayahara Nario 馬屋原成男, and Iida Yoshirō 飯田吉郎, who affixed Japanese readings to the Chinese characters used in the translation.

palace archives and survived the vicissitudes of political fortunes. In the late eighteenth century, Dutch medicine came to flourish in Japan and the old books on Chinese medicine were ignored further. Tamba's compilation consequently came to be revered only for its antiquity. It was published in Japan in 1860, 1906, 1909, and 1935 in limited editions and reprinted in 1955 on the Chinese mainland. This work was based entirely on ancient Chinese sources, but it was not until 1870 that the Chinese found out about it; it was then discovered by scholar Yang Shou-ching. Another Chinese scholar named Yeh Teh-hui came to Japan in 1902 and, while doing research in the former Imperial Library at Ueno, came across the twenty-eighth section of *The Essence of Medical Prescriptions* and noted that it cited valuable Chinese sources no longer extant. He extracted these citations and published them in 1903 as part of a compendium of rare Chinese sources.[4] The Western pioneer in this field was R. H. van Gulik, the eminent late Dutch sinologist. Dr. van Gulik translated many passages from Yeh Teh-hui's rearrangement, putting sexological descriptions into Latin, and made an extremely important contribution. He was the first Westerner to introduce these major writings on Taoist sexology to the general reading public and to explain their significance.[5]

The Essence of Medical Prescriptions fared well with the authorities, with the notable exception of its twenty-eighth section, concerning the bedroom arts. In 1906, when the complete work was published, the boudoir section was immediately prohibited and officially denounced as being injurious to social customs. The rest of the printing was not

---

4. For bibliographical details, see van Gulik, *Sexual Life in Ancient China* (Brill, 1961), pp. 122–23. Yeh Te-hui's 葉徳輝 compilation was called *Shuang-mei ching-an ts'ung-shu* 雙梅景闇叢書; in it he included reconstructions of five handbooks of sex found in the twenty-eighth section of *Ishimpō*. This portion of his work was made available in Japan in 1951 and 1964 through a Japanese translation, the second book a partial reprint of the first. (Nakayama Motosuke 中山素輔, tr., *Chūgoku Seishi. Sojokyō* 中國性史. 素女經, Tokyo, Murasaki Shobō 紫書房, 1951; *Shikido kimpishō* 色道禁秘抄, Tokyo, Hsinryūsha 新流社, 1964.)

5. Dr. van Gulik made many Chinese sexological sources available in *Sexual Life in Ancient China* and added valuable comments preceding and following his translations.

tampered with, but this section was removed. Only the first two volumes of the 1906 edition were printed. However, a new edition known as the *Asakuraya* was published in 1909 with the offending section in it, and it was overlooked by the authorities. No public library in Japan permitted readers to see the section on the bedroom arts, but it became even more widely known as a consequence. In the 1935 edition, passages in the twenty-eighth section, dealing with positions of intercourse and sexual techniques, were left blank. Many studies of the text were made surreptitiously by Japanese researchers in the late twenties and early thirties, when there was a mania for books on sex, but the materials were only partially understood. Imperfect understanding also characterized early Japanese studies regarding the aphrodisiacs and other types of medicines mentioned in the text.

The Essence of Medical Prescriptions is a medical survey of extraordinary value, based on ancient Chinese sources but not discovered by the Chinese until almost a thousand years after publication. This is but one example of how the Heian Japanese preserved Chinese sources and made available priceless materials for later ages.[6] The section on the bedroom arts is a collection of ancient comments on how to deal with sex within a set philosophical framework, and the tenor of its remarks is candid and factual. Despite the variety of source materials, these share a tendency to present statements without obfuscation, adhering to physiological descriptions. There is an impersonal quality to the writings, and extravagant descriptions of ecstatic feelings are avoided. The checkered fate of this text on the bedroom arts is an adequate comment in itself on the failure of the public official and the layman to make a

---

6. See H. S. Levy's translation of *Yu-hsien k'u* 遊仙窟, China's first novelette about sensual love, which was lost in T'ang China but brought to Japan and preserved there. (*The Dwelling of Playful Goddesses*, Dai Nippon Insatsu, Tokyo, 1965.) In a similar way, the Chinese did not find out about *Yu-hsien k'u* or *Ishimpō* until late in the nineteenth century. T'ang and Sung Chinese scholars must have been well aware of the export of some of their works. Ou-yang Hsiu, for example, wrote a poem in about 1060 in which he surmised that a complete edition of the *Book of Documents* (*Shu-ching* 書經) must have once been preserved in Japan. (Kojiro Yoshikawa, *An Introduction to Sung Poetry*, Harvard University Press, 1967, 10–12.)

distinction between serious studies of sex and those appealing mainly to pornographic or erotic fantasy. To the ancient Taoist, sex was a means to salvation, and he advocated that it be practiced in calm surroundings. The practitioner was cautioned never to forget that coitus was only a means to an end and that the end was health, well-being, and long life. The Taoists believed that the woman's emission was a loss to her but a gain for the man and, since the texts reflected the views of traditional male-oriented Chinese societies, most of the statements directed the male to secure physical enrichment at her expense. However, great attention had to be paid to the woman's feelings in order to get her to emit, and in this sense her status was improved. The Confucians may have considered woman to be a difficult and contrary being, a problem to bring up and control, but to the Taoists she was the repository of life and the source of well-being.

THE TAO OF SEX

CHAPTER I

Introduction

The twenty-eighth section of *The Essence of Medical Prescriptions*, appropriately called *Within The Bedroom*, has thirty chapters. The first chapter sets forth the fundamental principles of sexual intercourse, presenting its information in dialogue form. Each question is so phrased that the expert who responds to it can give his or her views in considerable detail; this is characteristic of subsequent chapters as well. The questions and answers that make up the text constitute a sort of " advice to the sex-lorn column," in which columnists and readers are members of a select Taoist circle. The Yellow Emperor, exalted as the sage-founder of Chinese medicine, answers some questions but asks others, proving that even a sage has problems with his sex life. When the discussion touches on ways to achieve longevity, expert opinion is elicited from P'eng Tsu, a Chinese venerable said to have lived more than nine hundred years. (We refer to him in our translation as " P'eng the Methuselah.") The Taoists were not averse to having feminine sex authorities; a series of women appear in this and later chapters, solving some problems and bringing up others. They have names such as the Woman Plain, the Woman Selective, and the Woman Profound; all are experts on the sexual arts, cited as early as the Han dynasty, who are called in as final arbiters. They have become Immortals and enjoy sagely status, the implication being that they reversed the process prescribed for males and had coitus with innumerable virgin youths until they reached the realm beyond old age and death. All questions in the first chapter about longevity are answered by P'eng the Methuselah, who asserts that to enjoy a prolonged life span a man should follow four courses of sexual action:

1. Maximize contact
2. Minimize leakage

15

3. Change women frequently

4. Have intercourse with virgins

Medical practitioners in ancient China considered the normal span of life to be a hundred years. The fact that a man deteriorated as early as fifty was due, they insisted, to his having failed to exercise restraint in his sex life. By this they meant that the man abandoned himself to passion and did not control the number of his emissions. Taoist doctors alleged that man further shortened his life by limiting himself to one woman and that men who knew the Way sought salvation in plurality. They weren't swayed by fine looks and seductive beauty, but chose women because they were young, amply fleshed, and childless. Each man was advised to treat feminine bed partners with the utmost care and to preserve his semen as he might life itself. The Taoists asserted it was essential for man to emulate the openings and closings of Heaven and Earth and to carry out coitus in order to diffuse the life-spirit. The life of the penis was in its movement without emission; if it failed to move, it would shrink and die.

When carried out in a mood of mental repose, sex was called a unifying force. To derive the greatest benefits from it, one had to know the proper bedroom sequence of male progressions and female reactions. A man who practiced sex out of the correct sequence ran the risk of getting sick and shortening his life. The efficacies of Chinese medicines are touched on in the closing chapters, but in this chapter it is unequivocally stated that all such medicines are useless unless one becomes adept in the bedroom arts.

The ancient Chinese divided physiology into contrasting aspects of air and blood. Since air corresponded to the male element and blood to the female element, it was believed that woman was made up of much blood and little air, while man had much air and little blood. In sexual terms, woman menstruated because she was blood-abundant, and during menstruation her blood became insufficient and her air increased. Since semen and blood were considered one in substance, it was essential for man to keep the little blood-semen he had and to try to supplement the supply through drawing in the woman's fluids. (The Chinese regarded all secretions of the uterus and vulva as constituting a woman's liquid essence.)[7]

---

7. van Gulik, *op. cit.*, p. 45.

Fundamental Principles

In *The Secrets of the Jade Bedroom*, the Master of Primordial Harmony said: "One female element and one male element— we call this the Way. Fertilizing the essence, converting it to life becomes its function. How far-reaching are its principles! Therefore, the Yellow Emperor questioned the Woman Plain, and P'eng the Methuselah answered the Yin dynasty King—these were significant transmissions. The Yellow Emperor asked the Woman Plain; "I have deteriorated in life-force and am out of harmony; within my heart is joylessness. My body is constantly apprehensive and imperiled. What shall I do about this?" The Woman Plain replied: "The reason for the decline of men is only that they all abuse the ways of female-male element intercourse. Now woman's superiority to man (in this respect) is like water's extinguishing fire. If you understand this and carry it out, you will be like the cauldrons and the tripods, which harmonize well the five flavors and thereby achieve a broth of meat and vegetables. These who know well the ways of the female and male elements achieve the five joys, while those who are ignorant of them shorten their lives. What pleasures and joys to be gotten! Can you fail to be cautious?" Then she said: "There is the Woman Selective, who has wondrously attained the techniques of the Way. The King (who is called the Yellow Emperor) sent the Woman Selective to ask P'eng the Methuselah about the ways of prolonging life and benefitting old age." Said P'eng: "One gets longevity by loving the essence, cultivating the spiritual, and partaking of many kinds of medicines; if you don't know the ways of intercourse, partaking of herbs is of no benefit. The producing of man and woman is like the begetting of Heaven and Earth. Heaven and Earth have attained the ways of intercourse and, therefore, they lack the limitation of finality. Man loses the ways of intercourse and he therefore has the mortification of early death. If you can avoid matters of mortification and injury and obtain the arts of sex, it will then become the way of non-death." The Woman Selective made a second obeisance and said, "I wish to hear about the essential teachings." Replied P'eng: "The Way is extremely easy to know; it is merely that man is unable to trust in it and practice it. The present ruler controls the government and rules the universe, but he cannot be knowledgeable in all of the ways. Fortunately, there are many in the harem, and it is suitable for him to know the methods of intercourse. The essential of the method is to have relations with many women while emitting semen infrequently. This causes one's body to be lightened and all illnesses to be reduced and eliminated."

The Shaman Tzu-tu, a Han dynasty Captain of the Royal Stables, was 138 years old when the Filial and Martial Emperor Hsiao-wu ti saw him while hunting above the Wei River. There was a strange vapor above his head, at a fixed elevation of ten feet or more. The Emperor marvelled at it and inquired about it, and Tung-fang Shuo replied, "This gentleman has a life-force whose far-reaching principles are in Heaven; he also has the art of conducting the female-male elements." His Highness had those about him withdraw, and he questioned Tzu-tu. Tzu-tu said: "Matters of sex are concealed in public. It is not suitable for me to speak, and those who can practice (my teachings) are few. That is why I don't dare to speak out. I received these arts from Tou Tzu-ming of Ling-yang when I was sixty-five and carried them out for seventy-two years. All who strive for longevity should seek this from the energy of life. To be greedy for feminine beauty and emit beyond one's vigor injures every vein and gives rise to every illness."

Designated Essentials of the Jade Bedroom states that P'eng the Methuselah said: "The Yellow Emperor controlled twelve hundred women and ascended as an Immortal. Ordinary people shorten their lives through having one woman. How can there not be a (great) distance between knowing and not knowing! Those who know the Way are merely distressed by the scarcity of women. All (such women) don't have to have fine looks and seductive beauty—one wishes only to secure types that are youthful and amply fleshed and have not yet fed (infants) from the breast. If you can get seven or eight, it is greatly beneficial." Said the Woman Plain: "In controlling your adversary, you should regard her as tile and stone and yourself as gold and jade. If your semen moves, you should quickly leave her vagina. Control a woman as you would a runaway horse with a rotten rope. Be as apprehensive as you might of falling into a deep hole filled with sword points. If you love your semen, your life will be indestructible."

The Yellow Emperor asked the Woman Plain, "I now wish to go for

a long time without intercourse; how should I go about it?" Replied
the Woman Plain: "You shouldn't do so. Heaven and Earth have
their openings and closings; there are changes in the workings of the
female and male elements. Man patterns himself after (the workings of)
these elements and is in accord with the four seasons. If you now wish
not to have intercourse, your life-spirit won't be diffused, and the female
and male elements will be closed off and separated. How will you then
augment yourself? Carry out a refinement of the life-force several
times, doing away with the old and taking in the new in order to help
yourself. If the jade stalk doesn't move, it will shrink and die. Reject
all reasoning about sex; practice special gymnastics. To be able to
move but not emit is the so-called returning of the semen. Supplement-
ing and benefitting the semen is then the way of the life-force."

The Classic of the Woman Plain states that the Yellow Emperor asked,
"Now, why should there be restraint in sexual intercourse?" Said
the Woman Plain: "From the first there has been a fixed order to the
method of sexual intercourse. The male arrives at non-deterioration,
and the female eliminates all illnesses. The heart rejoices and the life-
force vigor is strengthened. However, those who have intercourse in
ignorance gradually deteriorate and are thereby injured. If you wish to
know its ways, they are in settling the life-force, tranquilizing the mind,
and harmonizing the will. If the three phenomena are all attained,
your spirit is unified; neither cold or hot, hungry or satiated, your body
is regulated and fixed, and sex is always leisurely and relaxed. Shallow
insertions and leisurely movements, and few ins and outs; the woman
has pleasurable feelings, and the man flourishes and doesn't deteriorate.
Through this they attain their climax."

It is stated in *The Classic of the Woman Profound* that the Yellow
Emperor asked the Woman Profound, "I have received the sexual arts
from the Woman Plain and naturally have the method. Once more, I
wish to have you exhaust its ways (for me)." Said the Woman Profound: "Between Heaven and Earth, movement must (accord with)
the female and male elements. The male element gets the female one
and is converted; the female element gets the male one and is moved.
The female element and the male element must operate in mutuality.
Therefore, if the male (penis) feels, firm and strong, and the female
(vagina) moves, open and extended, two life forces exchange emissions

and flowing liquids penetrate mutually. The male has eight sequential progressions; the female has nine reactions. If in using them you lose the proper order, the male starts getting swellings and sores, and the woman harms her menstruation. All the illnesses arise and grow, and longevity is lost. If you are able to know its ways, you are delighted and strong, life is at once increased and extended, and your facial color is like that of an elegant blossom." In *Pao The Plain Master* it is said: "There are a myriad of medicines to be taken. (If you take these) and raise animals for nutrition as food but don't know the bedroom arts, there is no place where this will be beneficial. Because of this, the ancients feared man's trivial and wayward heart. Therefore, even though I explain this in detail, it can't be believed by all. Sexual interaction is comparable to water and fire. Water and fire kill man or benefit man, depending only on whether or not they can be used. If you are to grasp in general the essentials of the method, (it is that) in controlling women there is much benefit and good in numbers. If you are unenlightened in using its ways, one or two (women) are enough to hasten death." It also said: "If men cannot have intercourse (according to) the female and male elements, they then give rise to the disease of blood poisoning. Thus, forlorn and much troubled, they have many ailments and aren't long lived. Giving way to your feelings and relinquishing your intent also shorten life. You can be uninjured only by gaining a harmony (based on) suitable restraint."

The Master of the Cave Profound said: "Of the myriad things begotten by Heaven, man alone is the most precious. The place for man's being esteemed is in his moderation in sexual desire. He models Heaven, emulates Earth, adjusts to the female element, and conforms to the male element. Those who realize these principles cultivate their natures and prolong their years. Those who are contemptuous of its truths injure their spirits and prematurely shorten their years. You may proceed according to the methods of the Woman Profound and transmit them to distant posterity, but in stating fully the overall meaning you still cannot exhaust their profundities. I brought together the old rules and compiled this new book. Though I didn't investigate their purities, I did obtain the bare outlines. The forms of sitting, lying, stretching out, and crouching; the postures of lying upwards and lying downwards, opening and extending; the methods of side, rear, front, and back; the regulations for in and out, deep and shallow—all fit the principle for man-woman regulations and together they combine the number of the Five Elements.[8] Those who follow the Way will preserve long life as a consequence; those who transgress it fall into peril and dissolution. Since it already has profit for all of mankind, how can it not be transmitted for ten thousand generations?"

Recipes of Priceless Gold[9] said: " Man cannot be without woman, and woman cannot be without man. If you think of intercourse as isolated and alone, longevity is threatened and every ailment arises. Further, devilish apparitions rely on this to mix their semen (with the long-suffering woman), and the woman is injured by one demon as much as she would be by a hundred men." It also said: " Humans under thirty are often given to debauchery, while those over thirty experience their life-force vigor as being temporarily in decadence. In decadence a myriad of ailments swarm together. If over a long period these are not cured, in the end there's no help for them. Therefore, by the age of thirty you should be acquainted with the bedroom arts. Though their ways are extremely close at hand, people are unable to discover them. Their way is merely to control ten women a night without emitting semen. This concludes the bedroom arts. Combined with

8. The " Five Elements " constitutes an ancient Chinese philosophical theory which attempted to explain the universe as an interaction of natural phenomena. The elements were water, fire, wood, metal, and earth. Each of these was correlated with stars, seasons, colors, points of the compass, and the eight trigrams of the ancient Book of Changes. (van Gulik, *op. cit.*, p. 40n.) The " Five Elements " were also used to explain the ancient Chinese numerology which featured odd (male) and even (female) numbers from one to nine.

9. *Recipes of Priceless Gold* 千金方, composed by T'ang physician Sun Ssu-mo 孫思邈 (601–682), gave detailed observations on sex behavior. (van Gulik, *op. cit.*, 193–97.) It was incorporated into the *Tao-tsang* 道藏, the great compendium of Taoist writing, in 93 chapters, but in the Sung edition of 1066 it originally numbered 30 chapters. The author was said to have likened the preciousness of human life to a thousand pieces of gold, hence the title. (See the preface to *Recipes of Priceless Gold.*) Sun was later revered by Taoist believers as one who had achieved immortality. (*Ishimpō*, pp. 39–40.) Extracts from his book are to be found in *Yōjōkun* 養生訓 (See our annotated bibliography).

medicines, the life-force vigor, uninterrupted through the four seasons, is increased a hundredfold and wisdom is renewed daily."[10]

---

10.   In the original text, the section ends with the clause, " The art of this method " 此方之術也 ; it may be incomplete, with a concluding phrase omitted.

CHAPTER II

Introduction

The Taoists believed one nourished the male element by storing up the semen. They instructed the reader on how to do this, but warned him not to make this knowledge available to the female. What benefitted him was really injurious to her, so he was advised to get women who were innocent of the Way and to indoctrinate them so as to ensure his sexual well-being. He was told to try to secure virgins; they would transfer their energies to him and, if he could combine this transfer with non-emission, he might well be on the way to becoming a sage. The would-be semen-saver was instructed in a special mental concentration technique, somewhat reminiscent of Indian yoga,[11] through which he was to cause the semen to revert upwards through the center of the spinal cord and into the brain. Getting the semen to revert was of great concern to the Taoists, and the man on the verge of emission was instructed to change partners at once—" woman-changing can lengthen one's life." The second chapter concludes by describing ways to excite the woman, stressing kissing and tongue thrusts, giving in detail the physical signs which prove that she has become excited through sex play. The Taoists believed that a woman's saliva had curative properties, and they advised men to swallow as much of it as they could.

Nourishing the Male Element

The Secrets of the Jade Bedroom states that Chung the Master of

11. van Gulik, *op. cit.*, 339–59, has a detailed essay on Indian and Chinese sexual mysticism. He states that Chinese Taoist concepts stimulated the rise of Vajrayāna in India and that these concepts were later reimported into China twice.

Harmony said: "In the house where he nourishes the male element, (the man) does not let the woman look covertly upon these arts. Not only is it profitless to the male element, but it finally leads to injurious ailments. The so-called saying, 'If you lend a sharp object to someone (like a robber) he'll pull up his sleeves (prepared to fight),' leaves no room to doubt (that allowing women to steal these secrets will lead to trouble)."

He also states that P'eng the Methuselah said: "Now men who wish to obtain great benefits do well in obtaining women who don't know the Way. They also should initiate virgins (into sex) and their facial color will get to be like (the facial color of) virgins. However, (man) is only distressed by (a woman) who is not young. If he gets one above fourteen or fifteen but below eighteen or nineteen, it is even more beneficial and fine. However, the highest (number of years) must not exceed thirty. Those who, though not yet thirty, have already given birth cannot be beneficial (to the man). The masters preceding me who transmitted the Way to each other got to be three thousand years old. Those who combine this with medicines can get to be Immortals."

It is further said: "Those who practice the ways of sex and take in the life-force in order to cultivate longevity cannot do this through one woman (alone). If one gets three, nine, or eleven (women),[12] there is much benefit and good. He elects that his semen liquid revert to the Upper Vast Stream (of the brain cavity). His oily skin is glossy, his body light, his eyes clear, and his life-force strong and flourishing. He can subdue all (feminine) adversaries. Old men are as young in years as they were at twenty, and their vigor is increased a hundredfold."

It is further said: "In controlling a woman, when you are on the verge of being (emotionally) moved you should change her at once (for another). Woman-changing can lengthen your life. If, therefore, you revert to controlling (only) one woman, the woman's emission force

---

12. These odd numbers, all considered male-element numbers 陽數, accorded well with the effort to cultivate the male element at woman's expense. The pattern of numbers found on the back of an ancient tortoise was said to be female (*yin*), contrasted with the male (*yang*) numbers found on the back of ancient deer. The numbers were associated with the *Book of Changes* and the diagrams discovered in "The plan of the Yellow River and the book of the River Lo" (河圖洛書).

changes to a lesser one and the benefit is slight."

It is further stated that the Green Ox Taoist said: "If you change women often, many are the benefits. It is especially fine if you have more than ten partners a night. If you constantly control the same woman, her emission force changes to a weak one, which cannot greatly benefit the man. It also causes the woman to become emaciated."

The Secrets of the Jade Bedroom states that P'eng the Methuselah said: "The ways of sexual intercourse are not especially strange. But you should be composed and at tranquil ease, esteeming harmoniousness. You play with the cinnabar field about the pubic region, try to kiss her deeply, and thrust forward with the tongue and lightly glide with it in order to excite her. When a woman is moved by a man, there is evidence. Her ears get as hot as if she has drunk a strong wine; her breasts rise in warmth, and if you grasp them they fill your hands. The nape of her neck frequently moves, her legs are wildly brandished about, her licentious overflow appeals, and she presses on the man's body. At a time like this, if you draw back slightly and are shallow (in penetration), the penis gains the life-force and the female element is disadvantaged. Further, the liquids of the five viscera reside briefly in the tongue. The so-called 'Red Pine Master's'[13] jade fluids could thereby eliminate (the need for) the five cereals (because of the nutritious ingredients in the woman's mouth). During intercourse, if you take in a lot of tongue fluid and saliva, it will cause your stomach to become as purified as if you have drunk a medicinal broth. Diabetes is immediately cured and hot-headedness is lessened. Your skin is glossy, and your appearance is like that of a virgin. The Way is not far to discover, but common people are merely unable to recognize it." Said the Woman Selective, "By not going against human feelings, you can benefit in longevity. Is this not delightful?"

---

13. The Red Pine Master 赤松子 was an Immortal of the legendary era, associated with the Divine Agriculturist 神農. He was known as the Rain Controller 雨師, and it was said that he could go through fire without being burned. Because the Red Pine Master nourished himself on a jade fluid, this came to connote a wondrous substance like saliva, that might enable the imbiber to achieve immortality.

CHAPTER III

Introduction

This is the only chapter in our monograph on the bedroom arts which tells the woman how to join the Immortals by taking sexual advantage of the man. In one sense, the Taoists advocated equality of the sexes, for either could achieve immortality. They were much more liberal than the Confucianists in this regard.[14] One emancipated woman, the Queen Mother of the West, was an Immortal par excellence. The Yellow Emperor ascended to Heaven through unions with more than a thousand women; the Queen Mother duplicated his feat by taking in the semen of innumerable youthful and unknowing males. If a woman's blood was insufficient, it was believed she could replenish it from the excess blood of male youths, semen and blood being synonymous terms. The hapless male who had intercourse with the Queen Mother got sick from it, but she thrived and recaptured the bloom of youth. The woman who wanted to use sex to gain health and longevity had to turn the tables on the man by getting him agitated while keeping herself under control. She was advised to emulate the tranquility of the successful male; jealousy and outbursts of anger were strictly forbidden. So each sex symbolized to the other the way to long life and well-being, the struggle between them being to see if one could cause the other to emit. The end of the passage briefly alludes to intercourse with demons, but this is explained in much greater detail in the twenty-fourth chapter.

---

14. Dr. Joseph Needham noted that Taoist practices favorably influenced sex relations and elevated the woman's position in China. (*Science and Civilization in China*, vol. II, 146n.) Dr. van Gulik refers to an exchange of opinions he had with Dr. Needham on this matter, as a result of which he became convinced that his early unfavorable remarks about Taoist " sexual vampirism " had been unwarranted. (van Gulik, *op. cit.*, XIII.)

Nourishing the Female Element

The Secrets of the Jade Bedroom states that Harmony Master Chung said: "Not only should the male element be nourished, but the female element should likewise be. The Queen Mother of the West nourished the female element and got the Way. Once she had intercourse with a male, the male immediately became ill, but her facial color became shiny and glossy. She didn't wear face powder, often ate yogurt and cheese,[15] drew the five (musical) strings, harmonized her heart, and affixed her intent. She then caused herself to be without other desires." He also said: "The Queen Mother of the West had no husband, and she liked to have intercourse with virgin youths. Therefore, even though it's not a part of the world's (commonly known) teachings, how could it have been (known to) the Queen Mother alone?" (Anyone can do what she did by following the correct Way.)

He also said: "In having intercourse with a man, (the woman) should tranquilize her heart and settle her intent. If, for example, the male is not yet excited, you must wait till he becomes agitated. Therefore, control your feelings somewhat so as to respond in concert with him. In any event, you must not shake and dance about, causing your female fluid to be exhausted first. If it is exhausted first, since your body is emptied you therefore incur the illnesses of wind and cold. Or, hearing that the male has had intercourse with other women, you should repress and beware of the following, which are all (harmful manifestations): jealousy and grievous trouble; arousal of your female element life-force; rage, whether sitting or rising; emission of the fluid when you are alone; and becoming haggard and suddenly aging."

He also said: "If you know the way of nourishing the female element and cause the two life-forces to unite in harmony, you can convert this into a son. If you don't have a child, you can convert this into producing fluids to flow into the conduits of life energy. If you nourish the female element through the male element, a myriad

---

15. Chinese doctors believed that yogurt and cheese were extremely beneficial to one's health.

ailments are eliminated, your facial color is glossy, your skin is benefitted, years go by without your aging, and you always look youthful. If you thoroughly adhere to this way and constantly have intercourse with men, even when going nine days without eating you won't be aware of hunger. Sick (women) who have intercourse with devils get emaciated when they don't eat; in the case of intercourse with men, however, (women who don't eat don't get emaciated).

CHAPTER IV

Introduction

Ancient Chinese medical practice was predicated on a simple theory of nature, contrasting the natural aspects of Heaven and Earth with the physiological aspects of man. The man was modeled after Heaven, which revolved from the left, while the woman was patterned after Earth, which revolved from the right. These natural phenomena embodied precise principles for the realm of man. Humans who understood and followed such principles achieved the objectives of the bedroom arts, while transgressors inflicted injuries upon themselves. The fourth chapter contains a fairly detailed explanation of sexual positions for boudoir partners; the man's pressing downwards and the woman's moving upwards are rendered in Taoist metaphor as Heaven being pacified and Earth secured. Fondling and kissing are mentioned as the necessary preludes to sexual union. The man and woman suck in each other's saliva, bite each other's lips, and finger each other's ears. These techniques of sex play may have been prescribed in order to diminish feelings of bashfulness that might otherwise inhibit the woman prior to coitus. They also ensured that the man did not engage in intercourse too quickly, in total disregard of the woman's physiological needs. Here are further indications that, while the Confucians may have had the last word in family relations, the Taoists controlled the boudoir.[16]

This chapter stresses the importance of approaching sex in a harmonious and tranquil mood. You should endeavor, say the Taoists, to attain perfect equilibrium, impervious to extremes of heat or cold, satiation or starvation. To do otherwise is to invite nervous upset and impotence. The man does all of his sex play quite slowly and reduces withdrawals to a minimum. He is restrained and cautious, wishing to

---

16. van Gulik, *op. cit.*, p. 45.

take in the woman's saliva and her vaginal flow and to further increase his vitality by making his semen revert to the brain. Taoist and Confucian writers shared a liking for enumerations of natural and man-induced phenomena; concluding passages briefly allude to the five constancies, the seven injuries, and the nine factors. These are explained in detail in subsequent chapters.

Harmonizing the Will

The Master of the Cave Profound said: " Now Heaven rotates to the left, and Earth goes around to the right. Spring and summer fade, and autumn and winter inherit. The man chants and the woman harmonizes. The Above acts and the Below follows. These are the underlying principles of things and events. If the man shakes and the woman doesn't respond, or if the woman moves and the man doesn't follow, not only is there injury to the man, but there is also harm to the woman. This is because the male and female elements, in preceding and receding and in going up and down, have been turned about. If you have union in this way, it is profitless for both parties. Therefore, the man must always rotate to the left and the woman must go around to the right. The male charges downwards and the woman contacts upwards. If you have union in this way, it is called Heaven pacified and Earth achieved.

" The principles of dividing up deep and shallow, slow and quick, and east and west are not of a single Way, for there are myriad manifestations. For example, pushing gently like a small fish playing with a hook; pressing urgently like birds caught in the wind. Dragging forward and back, moving up and down, going and returning left and right, leaving and entering laxly and tightly—these are to be reciprocally esteemed and striven for. Approach these things with suitable control; you should not be obstinate and stupid. Musical notes thereby adopt their usefulness in accord with the times."

He further said: " In general, during the first intercourse the man sits on the woman's left and the woman sits on the man's right. Then the man sits on the ground with legs spread out V-wise and enfolds the woman to his bosom. He seizes her tiny waist and fondles her jade body; they speak of being intertwined and talk of being bound. Of one heart and one intent, they may embrace or grasp, their two forms drawn together, their two mouths mutually affixed. The man takes in the woman's lower lip; the woman takes in the man's upper lip. At the same time they suck one another's (lips) and feed on their saliva fluids. They may leisurely bite their tongues, slightly bite their lips, invite an embracing of heads, or press close and take (one another's) ears in their fingers. They soothe the above and pat the below, kiss to the left and sip to the right. Revealed are a thousand coquetries; done away with are a hundred reflections. He then has the woman take his jade stalk in her left hand, while he strokes her jade gate with his right hand. The male is consequently moved by the life force of the female element, and his jade stalk is excited to action. That condition is indeed vigorous, like a lone mountain peak soaring above and overlooking the Milky Way. The woman is moved by the life-force of the male element and the liquid of her cinnabar hole flows. That condition is indeed one of bubbling over, like a secluded stream discharging into a deep valley. These, then, are the sensations and the arousals caused by the female and male elements, something which cannot be achieved by human strength (alone). When excitement reaches this point, intercourse is permissible. If the man doesn't feel excitement or if the woman flows lewdly, these are both caused by an illness from within which is quickly manifested on the outside."

The Secrets of the Jade Bedroom states that the Yellow Emperor asked: " Now what of the ways of the female and male elements in intercourse? " The Woman Plain replied: " The ways of intercourse assuredly have forms and positions. The man thereby attains his life-force and the woman thereby eliminates illness. The heart's intent is achieved and the life-force vigor is benefitted and strengthened. Those who don't know the Way overdo it and deteriorate. If you want to know the Way, it is in pacifying the heart and harmonizing the will. The spirit reverts to a death state, neither cold, hot, satiated, or starved. You pacify the body and correct the intent; sex must be leisurely and slow, smoothly inserting and slowly moving, rarely exiting and entering. Through this one becomes restrained and cautious, not daring to transgress. Since the woman rejoices pleasurably, the man does not deteriorate."

It further states that the Yellow Emperor said: "Now I wish to force myself to have intercourse, but my jade stalk doesn't arise. I am embarrassed to my face and ashamed in my heart, and I perspire like a bead. Since my heart feels greedy with desire, I have forcefully assisted it with my hands. How can I thereby force this?" The Woman Plain replied: "What the Emperor inquires about is something which every man possesses. If you wish to have intercourse with a woman, assuredly there are principles to be observed. You must first harmonize the life-force, and the jade stalk will then arise. Obeying its five constancies, there are sensations in the nine parts. The woman has five colorations; you (should) fully ascertain their establishment. By gathering in your overflowing semen and by taking the fluid into your mouth, the semen's life-force returns and fills up your brain. You avoid the prohibitions of the seven ills and carry out the ways of the eight benefits. Your body, not going against the five constancies, can then be preserved. If your orthodox life-force is moribund within, every illness will disappear. The repositories of the viscera are peaceful and quiet and your skin shines, glossy and moist. Every time you have intercourse, there immediately arises lifeforce vigor a hundredfold, and your (feminine) adversaries submit. How can there be any shamefulness in this?"

The Designated Essentials of the Jade Bedroom states that the Taoist Liu Ching said: "In general, the way to control woman is first to strive to play and amuse gently, causing the spiritual (qualities) to harmonize and the intent to feel moved. After a good long while (of this), you can have intercourse and insert the jade stalk within. Strong and firm, suddenly withdrawing; make your entries and withdrawals relaxed and slow. Do not expel your semen (like dashing something down) from the heights. You'll upset the five viscera, injure the life-energy conduits, and give rise to every ailment as a consequence. Those, however, who do not emit in intercourse and in a day and a night have relations with several tens (of women) without losing their semen, completely cure all ailments and daily are benefitted in longevity."

The Classic of the Woman Profound states that the Yellow Emperor asked, "What should be done when the woman perchance is displeased during intercourse and, nature unmoved, doesn't eject fluid? The jade stalk is (then) weak, small, and vigorless." Replied the Woman

Profound: " The female and male elements respond only through being moved reciprocally. Therefore, if the female element can't be secured, the male element is displeased; if the male element can't be secured, the female element doesn't get excited. If the man wishes intercourse but the woman is displeased, or if the woman wishes intercourse but the man does not, their two hearts are not in harmony and they are not moved to emit. Furthermore, if you go up unexpectedly or go down suddenly (in emotion), the pleasures of love are not given. If the man wishes to seek the woman and the woman wishes to seek the man, their feelings and intent combine as one, and together they achieve delight at heart. Therefore, the woman's nature is stirred and moved, and the man's stalk flourishes. The man's vigor-mover manipulates the mouse in the empty boat,[17] and the emission fluid overflows. The jade stalk moves quickly or slowly, as it pleases, and the jade gate opens and closes, now empty, now full. Without effort the man will force his strongest adversary to flee the battle. Sucking in her emission, drawing in her life force, he irrigates her red chamber.[18] Now in revealing the nine factors, there are methods fully provided for in extending and contracting, looking up and down, going forward and back, bending and curving. The Emperor should carry out these (methods) in detail and be careful not to transgress or err."

---

17. The clitoris.
18. The uterus.

CHAPTER V

Introduction

Self-control being the prerequisite to boudoir control, the man is told that he must first become psychologically attuned. The writer goes on to describe one of the positions of coitus we shall read about later in the thirteenth chapter and in his description uses a series of metaphors to indicate positional relationships of the sexual organs. He writes in considerable detail, proceeding step by step. His analysis in depth serves as a valuable supplement to T'ang and pre-T'ang Chinese materials, which invariably refer to intercourse in vaguer and more indirect terms. The major emphasis in boudoir control is on the techniques the man should use to arouse and excite the woman. Some passages have such a contemporary ring to them that they might be citations from modern marriage manuals. The penis, when erect, is referred to as being " alive "; in Taoist metaphor, when it shrinks back to normalcy it is " dead." The man engaging in coitus is especially cautioned that, in order to avoid injuring himself, he should maintain the erection of his penis after the woman has had her orgasm. The technique in coitus of " nine shallow, one deep " is set forth in the next chapter.

Controlling the Boudoir

The Master of the Cave Profound said: " In general, when having intercourse for the first time you should first sit down and later lie down. The woman is on the left and the man is on the right. After lying down and getting settled, (the man) has the woman lie down, facing directly upwards; he extends her legs and spreads her arms. The man prostrates himself on top of her and kneels inside her thighs. At once he bestows the hardness of his jade stalk on the mouth of her jade gate. Deeply

34

luxuriant, like a reclining pine impinging on a deep valley, he further presses it in and out before her cave. He kisses her mouth and sucks her tongue; or he may look at her jade face above or her golden ditch[19] below. He fondles the space between her belly and breasts and strokes the side of her jade terrace.[20] With this, in feelings the man is already bewitched, and in intent the woman is truly infatuated. Then with his virile point he attacks in every direction, charging the vein of jade below[21] or pinching the golden ditch above. He pierces below her royal college[22] and rests to the right of her jade terrace. The woman's lewd fluid fiills the cinnabar hole to its brim, and at once it quickly leaks its essence. At this time the virile point is plunged into the womb. He joyfully emits his semen and their fluids flow together, irrigating the god fields above and the solitary valley below.[23] When (the penis) is made to come and go, venturing forth in attack, and when it is made to advance and retreat, rubbing and scouring, the woman invariably seeks death and life and begs for sex and destiny. Then, after drying it and wiping it off with a cloth, he takes the jade stalk and plunges it deeply into the cinnabar hole till it reaches the sun terrace.[24] It is rugged, like a great rock embracing a deep valley. Then he carries out the " nine shallow, one deep " technique, and with this leans vertically and loiters horizontally, pulling nearby and drawing out alongsides. Sometimes he is leisurely or quick, at other times he is deep or shallow.

" Experiencing (the time needed to take) twenty-one breaths, he awaits the exiting and entering of the life-force, and the woman gets a pleasurable feeling. The man then rapidly inserts and quickly pierces; he pierces in and out, elevating his waist. He awaits the woman's agitation and adapts the slowness and quickness (of his movements) accordingly. In other words, with the virile point he attacks her grain seed,[25] inserts it into her womb, and grinds and rubs left and right. If

---

19. The upper part of the vulva.
20. The clitoris.
21. The place below the vulva where the labia meet.
22. The left and right sides of the vulva.
23. Preputium clitoridis and fossa vestibuli vaginae.
24. Glandula vestibularis major.
25. Glans clitoridis.

he himself is untroubled, and if he minutely pulls it up and draws it out, the woman's emission fluid should overflow. The male should then withdraw; he cannot revert to death but must return to life. A death-like emission is largely injurious to the male. One should be especially cautious (to remove the penis from within the vagina while it is still hard).

The Classic of the Woman Plain states that the Yellow Emperor asked, " Do you esteem the methods of the female-male elements? " Replied the Woman Plain: " When you are about to control a woman, first you order her to slacken her hands, relax her body, and bend both legs. The man enters between them, holds her mouth in his mouth, and sucks her tongue. He pats and guides his jade stalk and strikes both the east and west sides of her gate. For about the space of a single meal, he leisurely inserts his jade stalk. The fat and robust should insert it one and half inches,[26] the thin and weak one inch. Do not move it agitatedly. If you slowly take it out and again insert it, you will eliminate every ailment. Do not cause it to leak out on the four sides. When the jade stalk enters the jade gate, it naturally produces heat and, further, is quick. The woman's body naturally should move and be agitated; thus, she naturally secures (satisfaction) with the male. Afterwards, when he enters deeply, every male and female ailment can be eliminated. Piercing the lute strings[27] in a shallow way, if you insert it three and a half inches, you should close your mouth (to decrease excitement) and pierce her. Count from one to nine (to distract yourself); afterwards, deepen the penetration and on reaching the side of the mixed rock[28] go back and forth. Your mouth touches the woman's mouth; breathing in the woman's energy, practice the way of the nine-nine. It should finally be like this.

---

26. This was a special body measurement, referring to the practitioner's own body. It designated the length between the first and second joint of the practitioner's own finger when it was in a bent position. This constituted the " one inch " referred to in our text, with the man measuring the thumb on his left hand and the woman the thumb on her right hand. This system of measurement is still used today in acupuncture to determine the depth or shallowness of needle insertions. (*Ishimpō*, 62–63 n.)
27. Frenulum clitoridis.
28. Glandula vestibularis major.

CHAPTER VI

Introduction

The man is advised first to get the woman relaxed; he is told once again to be slow and unhurried in his insertions and to prevent leakage. He is instructed to count, probably to distract himself from the sexual drive towards completion and to ensure that he doesn't get too involved in the act. The inference to be drawn from this and similar Taoist discourses on the bedroom arts is that a man should not abandon himself to desire but follow instead set procedures that automatically induce a form of self-repression.

The Five Constancies are traditionally associated with the constant Confucian virtues of benevolence, righteousness, propriety, knowledge, and sincerity, but here we are provided with a sex interpretation. But for the fact that the Taoists are so deadly serious about sex, we might suspect this interpretation to be a parody of the Confucian enumeration. The Confucians revere the constancy of man; the Taoists revere the constancy of the penis. For the penis, too, has its five constancies, namely:

1. Restraint: not acting impetuously, even when it resides in the feminine depths.

2. Virtue: being able to carry out everything because it cherishes virtue in the extreme.

3. Benevolence: the intent of the penis in giving to others; in other words, the state of erection.

4. Duty: a philosophical connection is drawn between duty and the way the penis is constituted. There is duty in the emptiness within, referring to the penis' being formed from a spongy substance.

5. Propriety: regarding as chaste the glands which, though in a state of extreme expansion, during coitus rise and lower as they please.

The penis is also praised for being trustworthy and wise. It remains

37

steadfast during intercourse and is constant to the tenet of non-emission. As a consequence, man achieves longevity and rids himself of illness.

The Five Constancies

The Secrets of the Jade Bedroom states that the Yellow Emperor asked, " What do the Five Constancies mean? " Replied the Woman Plain: " The jade stalk truly possesses the way of the Five Constancies. Residing deeply in the place of the female element, it holds to restraint and protects itself. Within, it cherishes extreme virtue, and there is nothing that it does not succeed in carrying out. Now the intent of the jade stalk when it is about to bestow is benevolent. To have an emptiness in its midst is righteousness. To have restraint in extremity is propriety. To arise when wishing to and to stop when not wishing to is trustworthiness. To approach the matter of lowering and raising is wisdom. Because of this, the Man of Verity[29] relies on the Five Constancies for restraint. Though you want to carry out benevolence, if your semen is distressed and not firm (you can't accomplish it). As for righteousness, in protecting its emptiness you should clearly prohibit and not allow the getting of an abundance (of semen). This is truly the way already prohibited. Further, you should carry out intercourse with propriety, forming a restraint. Holding to truth and maintaining it, trustworthiness then becomes manifest. Thus should you realize the ways of intercourse. Therefore, if you obey the Five Constancies you will achieve longevity."

---

29. The Man of Verity 真人 here refers to the Taoist who has achieved religious perfection; it is a term found in pre-Han philosophic writings. (The same term in Buddhism signifies an Arhat who embodies truth; in other words, a Buddha.) The Taoist Man of Verity achieved immortality through his realization of the profoundest meanings of the Tao.

CHAPTER VII

Introduction

These are the five signs a man should look for to ascertain if the woman is ready for intercourse. For each sign that she gives, the man is instructed to take appropriate action. Ancient Chinese society was male-dictated; here and throughout the text the male viewpoint is given. Woman becomes an instrument for man to play upon in accord with the Taoist boudoir laws. Her reddened face is a sign that she is ready for intercourse; when she perspires and her breasts harden, these are signs that the penis should be inserted; the dryness of her throat is a signal for the male to excite her unhurriedly still futher; the slipperiness of her vagina is a sign that the penis can be inserted still deeper; finally, her having an emission is a sign for the man to withdraw.[30]

The Five Signs

The Secrets of the Jade Bedroom states that the Yellow Emperor asked, " How can I become aware of the joyfulness of the woman? " Replied the Woman Plain: " There are five signs, five desires, and ten movements. By looking at these changes you'll become aware of the reasons for them. Now as for the awaiting of the five signs, the first is called ' face reddened '; then leisurely unite with her. The second is called ' breasts hard and nose perspiring '; then leisurely insert the jade stalk. The third is called ' throat dry and saliva blocked'; then leisurely agitate her. The fourth is called ' the vagina is slippery '; then leisurely go in more deeply. The fifth is called ' the buttocks transmit fluid '; then leisurely draw (the fluid) out (from her).

---

30. van Gulik, *op. cit.*, 156, notes that these signs agreed in detail with those listed by Kinsey in *Sexual Behavior of the Human Female.*

CHAPTER VIII

Introduction

Here the Taoists set forth ways for the man to discern whether the woman wants sex. The external changes she goes through make manifest her spiritual and physical desires and her experience of orgasm. She takes shorter breaths and her nose and mouth dilate; one possible implication of our text, though unexpressed, is that when this occurs the man should try to adjust his rhythm to hers. There is a change in her facial expression, signified by rigidity or contraction of the facial muscles. She also reacts when the man holds back on emitting his semen. On the verge of orgasm she perspires profusely, and at its apex her arms and legs become rigid. The Taoists who compiled the sources cited in our text must have based their comments on fairly close observation, proceeding in a spirit of scientific inquiry to record what they had either heard about or seen.

The Five Desires

The Woman Plain said: "Through the five desires, one is made aware of the woman's response. The first is called 'intent'; about to obtain this, her breath is bated and her energy is withheld. The second is called 'sex awareness'; about to obain this, her nose and mouth are dilated. The third is called 'acutely aware'; about to be overcome by passion, excited and agitated, she embraces the male. The fourth is called 'concentration'; on the verge of fullness, perspiration flows and dampens her dress. The fifth is called 'joyfulness'; on the verge of extremity, her body straightens and her eyes close."

CHAPTER IX

Introduction

The chapter describes the physical methods by which the woman cleaves to the man. First, she embraces him with both hands and tries to get their sexual organs to touch. Then she rubs her thighs against his thighs, extends her belly when about to emit, and moves her buttocks. Wishing to deepen the penetration of the penis, she raises her legs and adheres to the man with them. Then she crosses her legs, to relieve the itching sensation she feels within. She may also shake her body from side to side, raise it to exert more pressure on the man, and extend herself prior to emission. In the boudoirs of the rich, there must have been many helping hands; several descriptions in the thirteenth chapter make it clear there were times when three in intercourse were not a crowd. The threesome perhaps provided the setting for close observation by one of the participants and information for the ancient sexologist. Perhaps on such occasions a non-participant observer noted the woman's mental and physical reactions.

The Ten Movements

Said the Woman Plain: "As for the effect of the ten movements, the first is called ' to embrace the man with both hands and want the bodies to cleave together and the sexual parts to touch.' The second is called ' to extend both thighs, urgently rubbing the upper side of the thighs.' The third is called ' to compress the belly, about to leak (fluids).' The fourth is called ' for the buttocks to move in joyful goodness.' The fifth is called ' to raise both legs and adhere to the man (with them), wishing (the penetration) deeper.' The sixth is called ' to cross over both thighs, inwardly itching lewdly.' The seventh is

41

called ' to shake to the sides, wishing that it deeply slice left and right.' The eighth is called ' to raise her body to press the man, the extreme of lewd amusement.' The ninth is called ' to stretch her body lengthwise, bodily parts joyful.' The tenth is called ' for the vagina fluid to be slippery, the essence having already leaked out.' Seeing these effects, you then become aware of the woman's joys."

CHAPTER X

Introduction

The four attainments refer to the attainments of the penis when it becomes swollen, corpulent, hard, and hot. A series of correspondences are conceptualized, with each of the physical changes in the condition of the penis likened to either mental or physical attributes: harmony, skin, bones, and spirit. Then the semen is similarly analyzed in terms of its four attainments. First, there is the dawning, in which sexual desire buds and the penis gradually becomes elevated. Next, there is the beginning, which probably means a further elongation of the first stage. The third stage is the shutting off of the semen; in the fourth and final stage, the emission exit for the semen refers to the aperture of the penis. In other words, when the libido reaches its climax and semen is about to be emitted, through a force of will the passageway is closed off and ejaculation is prevented. Once again we are informed of the non-ejaculation ideal of the male practitioner of the bedroom arts.

The Four Attainments

The Classic of the Woman Profound states that the Yellow Emperor said, " I mentally covet intercourse but my stalk doesn't arise. Can I compel its use?" Replied the Woman Profound, " You cannot. Now the way of desiring intercourse is for the male to pass through four attainments in order to get the nine essences of the woman." Asked the Yellow Emperor, " What is the meaning of the four attainments?" Replied the Woman Profound: " If the jade stalk isn't angry, the harmonious essence is not attained. If it is angry but not large, the fatness essence is not attained. If it is large but not hard, the bone essence is not attained. If it is hard but not hot, the spiritual essence

43

is not attained.   Therefore, anger is the dawning of the sperm; largeness is the beginning; hardness is the shutting off; and hotness is the gate. The four essences attained, restrain them through the Way.   In opening an opportunity, don't be rash; in opening the semen, don't leak."

CHAPTER XI

Introduction

The nine essences of the woman come into play after the man has completed the four attainments mentioned in the preceding chapter. They constitute the ways in which the woman participates in coitus. First, she takes long breaths and salivates, indicating an increase in the number of breaths and an excessive secretion of the salivary glands. These are the initial physiological signs that she is preparing for coitus. Next, she cries out and kisses the man, making sounds and movements which, according to the Taoists, reflect changes in the heart muscle and the blood vessels. She goes a step further and embraces the man, a heightening of excitement centered in activities of the spleen. Then, as her libido is stimulated, secretions take place in the vagina. The text refers to these as being an emanation from the kidneys, because in ancient Chinese medicine the kidneys were considered the source of the generative organs. She then graduates to an orgasm, evidenced by the way she gnaws at her mate. With this reaction, her passivity and shyness vanish, and she becomes increasingly aggressive. Once her blood and flesh are totally aroused, she plays unashamedly with the parts of the man's body susceptible to sexual arousal. The text mentions the five viscera: namely, the liver, heart, spleen, lungs, and kidneys, which make themselves manifest by affecting muscles, blood, flesh, skin, and bones.

The Nine Essences

The Classic of the Woman Profound states that the Yellow Emperor said, " How good they are! The nine essences of woman—how can one become aware of them? " Replied the Woman Profound: " Examine these nine essences in order to learn about them. When a woman takes great breaths and swallows her saliva, the lung essence has arrived. When she cries out and sucks the man, the heart essence has arrived. When she embraces and holds him, the spleen essence has arrived. (With) the slippery dampness of the gate of the vagina, the kidney essence has arrived. When she excitedly gnaws the man, the bone essence has arrived. When she hooks the man with her feet, the muscle essence has arrived. When she fondles and plays with the jade stalk, the blood essence has arrived. Holding and playing with the man's teats, the flesh essence has arrived. When you have intercourse with her for a long time and play with her seed,[31] in order to realize her intentions, the nine essences have all arrived. If (the essences) do not arrive, (the woman) will be harmed. Therefore, when this happens (one should) carry them out by (sequential) number in order to remedy this."

---

31. The clitoris.

CHAPTER XII

Introduction

This is the first of six chapters to describe varied positions of man and woman in sexual intercourse. As already noted, the monograph first explains in detail the need to achieve a proper mental state before practicing the bedroom arts. Once the will is in harmony, one shifts from spiritual preparation to physical action. The techniques in this chapter are named after the actions of animals. Almost all of them are duplicated in the next chapter, which expands the number of positions from nine to thirty, but the style of writing here is more descriptive. Almost invariably the positions as described are normally achievable and they do not require gyrations or acrobatics. These positions are esteemed as secrets among secrets. The Yellow Emperor is instructed in them by the Woman Profound, after he has promised to conceal them in the Stone House Library, where treasures are stored, and never to make the revelations public. The titles of the positions are made up of metaphors that describe motions of intercourse: the fluttering and flying of a dragon; the tread of a tiger; the spring of a monkey; the clinging of a cicada to a tree trunk; a tortoise mounting; a phoenix in flight; a rabbit sucking; two fish mutually attached, like Siamese twins; and two cranes whose long necks are intertwined. The man is always the one to take the initiative, making the woman assume the desired pose; and he is the one to benefit.

The Nine Ways

The Classic of the Woman Profound states that the Yellow Emperor said: " I have heard of the nine ways but not of how these ways (are practiced). I wish you to state these for me, in order to reveal their intent. I shall conceal this (commentary) in the Stone Room[32] and practice its ways."

Replied the Woman Profound: "The first of the nine ways is called, 'the dragon turns over.' Cause the woman to lie down facing directly upwards; the male lies on top of her, his thighs pressing on the mat.[33] The woman raises her vagina and thereby receives the jade stalk. He pricks her grain seed and attacks her from above. He moves about leisurely, eight shallow and two deep. Death goes and life returns, and his vigor flourishes and is intensified. The woman is flustered and pleased, and her joy is like that of a songstress (in the throaty sounds she makes). She naturally closes and firms, and the hundred ailments vanish.

龍　翻

（九法第一）

32. The Stone Room 石室 refers to a very carefully sealed room in which precious writings were stored; the term already meant this as early as the Han dynasty. The passage in our text shows that the transmission of esoteric knowledge about the right ways to have intercourse was regarded as a secret to be guarded carefully and never divulged to outsiders. Ancient medical knowledge and mystic concealment were related terms, showing the association of medicine with sacred religious concepts.

33. In T'ang times, a low bed was placed in the bedroom for one to sit on or lie upon. It was made of wood, as indicated by Heian picture scrolls.

" The second is called ' the tiger's tread.' Have the woman face downwards in a crawling position, buttocks up and head down. The male kneels behind her and embraces her belly. He then inserts the jade stalk and stabs it exceedingly within her. He strives to make it deeply intimate. They go back and forth in mutual pressure; if carried out to the numbers of five and eight, the (proper) degree is naturally obtained. The woman's vagina is closed and extended, and when her emission fluid overflows outwards (the intercourse) is ended and you rest. The hundred ailments do not arise, and the male prospers increasingly.

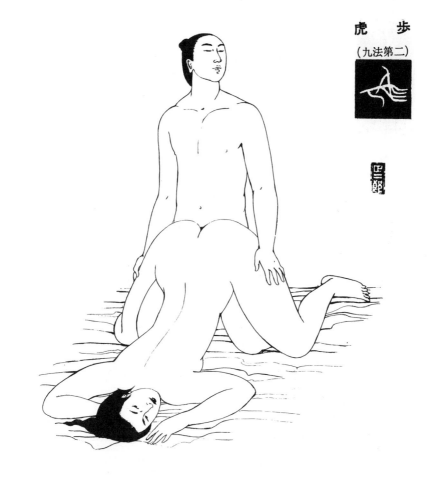

虎　歩
（九法第二）

"The third is called 'the monkey springs.' Have the woman lie down; the man supports her thighs. Her knees still go past her chest and her buttocks and back are simultaneously raised. He then inserts the jade stalk and pierces her odoriferous mouse.[34] The woman is bothered and agitated, and her emission fluid is like rain. If the man presses down deeply, (his penis) becomes vigorous and angered. When the woman rejoices, he ceases. The hundred ailments are naturally cured.

猿　　搏

（九法第三）

---

34. The vaginal secretion.

" The fourth is called ' cicada affixed.'   Have the woman lie kneeling downwards and extend her body straight out.   The man kneels behind her and inserts the jade stalk deeply.   He raises her buttocks slightly in order to tap at her red pearl,[35] carrying out (movements in time with) the numbers six and nine.   The woman is excited, and her emission flows.   Urgently moved within her vagina, she opens it to the outside. When the woman rejoices, he ceases.   The seven ills are naturally eliminated.

蟬　附

（九法第四）

---

35.   Labium minus pudendi.

" The fifth is called ' the tortoise mounts.' Have the woman lie down straight and bend her two knees. The man then pushes these (until) her feet reach her teats. He inserts the jade stalk deeply and pierces the infant girl.[36] Through deep and shallow measures he causes (his penis) to strike her seed. The woman then feels pleasurable and her body naturally shakes and lifts. When her emission fluid overflows, he then inserts it to the deepest extremity. When the woman rejoices, he ceases. In carrying this out, don't lose your semen and your vigor will increases a hundredfold.

龜　騰

（九法第五）

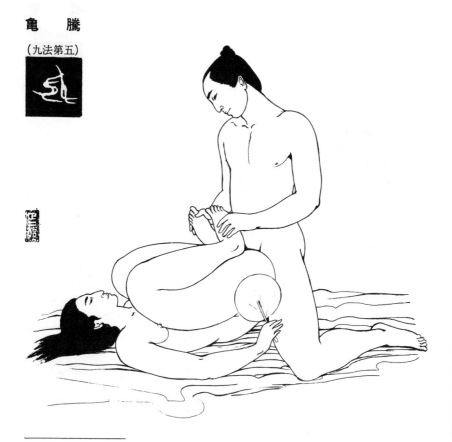

36. Glandula vestibularis major.

" The sixth is called ' the phoenix flutters.' Have the woman lie
down straight, raising her legs herself. The man crawls between her
thighs and, with both hands on the mat, he deeply inserts the jade stalk
and pierces her mixed rock.[24] Hard and hot he guides it in, and has
her move about so as to carry out the numbers three and eight. When
their buttocks suddenly press close, the woman's vagina opens and
naturally spits forth emission fluid. When the woman rejoices, he
ceases. The hundred ailments are gotten rid of.

鳳　翔

（九法第六）

" The seventh is called ' a rabbit sucking a hair.' The man lies down exactly in the reverse direction, extending his legs straight out. The woman straddles him from above, her knees to the outside. The woman's rear and head face his feet; she holds on to the mat, head down. He then inserts the jade stalk and stabs her lute strings.[27] The woman rejoices, and her essence fluid flows out like a stream. Rejoicing and happiness move (her to a) divine appearance. When the woman rejoices, he ceases. The hundred ailments will not arise.

兎 吮 毫

（九法第七）

" The eighth is called ' fish with scales joined.' The man lies straight down and the woman straddles him from above, her thighs facing forwards. He easily and quietly inserts the jade stalk, enters slightly, and then stops. Let it be received just a bit and don't (penetrate) deeply, like a child at its mother's breast. Cause the woman to move and strive alone, and have her prolong this. When the woman rejoices, the man withdraws. It cures all harshness of temperament or function.

魚 接 鱗

（九法第八）

" The ninth is called 'cranes with necks intertwined.' The man sits in a squatting position, the woman bestride his thighs. She embraces his neck with her hands; (he) inserts the jade stalk, stabs her wheat buds,[37] and strives to strike her seed. The male embraces the woman's buttocks and assists her upward movements. The woman naturally feels joyful and her essence fluid overflows. When the woman is joyful, he ceases. The seven ills are naturally cured."

鶴 交 頸

（九法第九）

---

37. Labium minus pudendi.

CHAPTER XIII

Introduction

This chapter quotes The Master of the Cave Profound and outlines thirty positions of sexual intercourse which it alleges represent the extent of variations on the coitus theme. One can infer from the Preface that explanatory diagrams were appended to the original work. The nine positions of the previous chapter are almost all duplicated. The first four positions listed are used in pre-coital play. The description of these positions was abridged because they were already given in the chapter on harmonizing the will. These thirty positions provided the nucleus for the much later amplification in the Tokugawa era of the " forty-eight skills." However, the thirty positions differ from many of the Tokugawa aplifications in that they require a minimum of acrobatics. The positions in this chapter are depicted through a series of metaphors; animals move certain ways in the sky and on earth, ways peculiar to them and relevant to what the author is trying to convey. There are joinings, soarings, and intertwinings, and love-mates are described as same hearted and inseparable. Only the last of the thirty positions, in which man and woman connect rear to rear, seems to be a physical impossibility. The title of the last position, referring to a dog in three different periods of autumn, may allude to a belief among the ancients that in autumn dogs copulated in the way the text describes. Three of the thirty positions include a third party, indicating the polygamous nature of Chinese royalty and arisocracy and the prevalence and availability of servants. In one instance, the woman uses two men, implying that powerful women of eminent clans may have indulged their lustful desires as they pleased.

The Thirty Ways

The Master of the Cave Profound said: " Examining the postures of intercourse, there are no more than thirty ways.   Among them there are crooking or extending; looking down or up; going out or in; being shallow or deep; but these are largely similar and only slightly different. They can be said to be completely concealed and unspoken, but (here) I shall take them up one and all, model their postures, and record their names.   I shall avail myself of their forms in order to set up their designations.   Intimate friends and gentlemen, exhaust the wondrousness of their intent.

1.   Entanglement Revealed
2.   Attachment Inseparable
3.   Exposed Fish Gill
4.   Unicorn Horn

The four postures above, postures of external amusements, are all of the first rank.

5. Silkworm Reeling Silk

The woman lies down on her back; with both hands poised upwards, she embraces the man's neck and entwines both legs about his back. The man, embracing the woman's neck with two hands, kneels between her thighs and inserts the jade stalk.

蚕 纏 綿

（卅法第五）

6. Shifting-Turning Dragon

The woman lies down on her back, bending both legs. The man kneels within the woman's thighs and pushes both her legs forward with his left hand, causing them to go past her breasts. He takes the jade stalk with his right hand and inserts it into the jade gate.

7. Fish Eye-to-Eye

The man and woman lie down together. The woman places one leg over the man; they are face to face, sucking mouths and sipping tongues. The man extends both legs, supports the woman's upper leg with his hand, and advances the jade stalk.

魚 比 目

（卅法第七）

8. Heart-Sharing Swallows

Have the woman lie on her back and extend her legs.   The man rides the woman, crouches on her belly, and embraces her neck with both hands. The woman embraces the man's waist with both hands, and he inserts his jade stalk into her cinnabar hole.[38]

燕 同 心

（卅法第八）

---

38. The vagina.

9. Kingfishers Intertwined.

Have the woman lie on her back with legs raised. The man does a barbarian squat,[39] opens the woman's legs, and sits amidst her thighs. He embraces her waist with both hands and advances his jade stalk amidst her lute strings.[27]

翡 翠 交

（卅法第九）

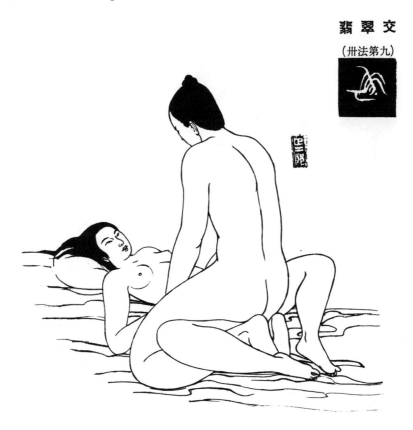

---

39. The term "barbarian squat" 胡跪 refers to a method of sitting by non-Chinese peoples in which one placed one's right knee on the ground and sat with one's weight shifted to the left knee. It was considered a reverential seating posture. (See the *Morohashi* dictionary, description following 胡跪.)

10. Joined Mandarin Ducks

Have the woman lie down on her side, raising both legs and resting
them on the man's thighs. Behind the woman's back, the man rides
above her lower legs. He straightens out one knee, places it on the
woman's upper thigh, and inserts the jade stalk.

鴛鴦合

（卅法第十）

11. Sky-Soaring Butterfly

The man lies on his back with both legs extended, and the woman sits on top of him, face to face. Her feet hold to the mat. Then with her hands she assists his vigor and advances his male tip into the jade gate.

12. Rear-Flying Wild Duck

The man lies on his back with both legs extended. The woman sits on the man, back to face. The woman's legs hold to the mat and she lowers her head, embraces the man's jade stalk, and inserts it into the cinnabar hole.

背 飛 鳧

(卅法第卆)

13. Recumbent Covered Pine

Have the woman cross her legs and face upwards. The man embraces the woman's waist with his hands, and the woman embraces the man's neck with hers. He inserts the jade stalk within the jade gate.

偃 蓋 松

(卅法第圭)

14. Bamboos Converging on The Altar

The man and woman stand together, face to face. They suck mouths and embrace. (He) takes his male point and injects it deeply into the cinnabar hole; as it arrives within the sun terrace, it is completely submerged.

臨 壇 竹

（卅法第卤）

15.   The Paired Dance of the Female Phoenixes
A man and (two) women, one lying on her back and one lying on her
stomach.   The one on her back raises her legs, the one on her stomach
rides on top.   Their two vaginas face one another.   The man sits
cross legged, displaying his jade thing, and attacks (the vaginas) above
and below.

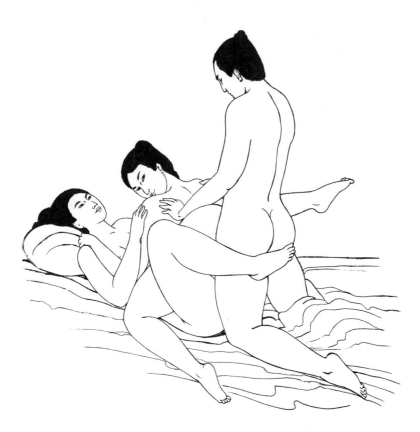

16.   The Phoenix Takes (Two) Fledgelings

When the woman is big and fat, she uses a small male (in addition). If they have intercourse with her together, it greatly excels (the usual way).

17.   The Seagull Soars

The man approaches the side of the bed,[40] lifting up the woman's legs in order to make them elevated.   The man inserts his jade stalk into her womb.

海 鷗 翔

(卅法第七)

---

40.   The bed referred to here must have been high enough for the man to stand by its side and manipulate the woman's legs as directed.   This position would have been impossible to achieve on the low bed customarily used by the T'ang Chinese and the Heian Japanese.

野 馬 躍

（卅法第大）

18.   The Wild Horse Leaps

Have the woman lie on her back.   The man lifts up the woman's legs and puts them on his shoulders, left and right.   He deeply inserts the jade stalk into the jade gate.

野 馬 躍

（卅法第六）

19. Fast-Stepping Steed

Have the woman lie down. The man squats; with his left hand supp-
orting the woman's neck and his right hand lifting up the woman's
leg, he inserts his jade stalk into her womb.

驥 騁 足

（卅法第尢）

20. The Horse's Shaking Hooves

Have the woman lie down. The man lifts up one of the woman's legs and places it on his shoulder. The other leg naturally raises, and he inserts the jade stalk deeply within the cinnabar hole. How greatly interesting this is!

馬 揺 蹄

（卅法第廿）

21. The White Tiger Jumps

Cause the woman to lie face downwards, knees drawn up. The man crawls behind the woman, both hands embracing her waist, and inserts the jade stalk within the womb.

白 虎 騰

（卅法第三）

22. Dark Affixed Cicada

Have the woman lie face downwards and extend her legs. The man is within her thighs. He bends his legs, embraces the woman's neck with both hands, and from behind inserts the jade stalk within the jade gate.

玄 蟬 附

（卅法第三）

23. Mountain Goat Facing A Tree

The male sits with legs outspread and has the woman sit on him with her back to his face. The woman lowers her head herself and looks at the jade stalk being inserted. The man suddenly embraces the woman's waist and thrusts roughly.

山羊対樹

（卅法第三）

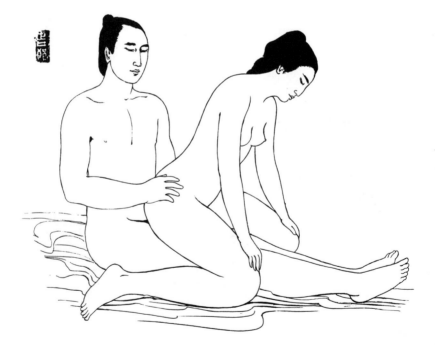

24. Gamecock and Fowl Approach The Arena

The man does a barbarian squat, on the mat. He has a young maid servant embrace his jade stalk and insert it into the (other) woman's jade gate. The one woman pulls at the (other woman's) robe from behind, to make her legs quicken; how greatly interesting this is!

25.   A Phoenix Frolics at Cinnabar Hole

Have the woman lie on her back, raising her legs herself with both her hands.   The man kneels behind the woman, holding to the mat with his two hands, and inserts the jade stalk into the cinnabar hole. This is superlatively excellent.

丹穴鳳遊

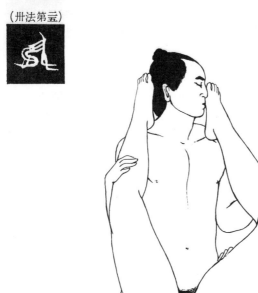

26. A Great Bird Soars Over a Dark Sea

Have the woman lie on her back. The man takes both of her legs and places them over his upper arms, left and right. With his hands in a downwards direction, he embraces the woman's waist and then inserts the jade stalk.

27. Wailing Monkey Embracing A Tree

The man sits with legs outspread, and the woman rides on his thighs.
She embraces the man with both hands, and he supports her buttocks
with one hand and inserts the jade stalk.   With the other hand he holds
on to the mat.

吟猿抱樹

（卅法第宅）

28. Cat and Rat Share a Hole

The man lies on his back, with feet extended. The woman crouches on top of the man and deeply inserts his jade stalk. Further, the man (may) crouch on the woman's back and attack the jade gate with his jade stalk.

猫鼠同穴

（卅法第元）

29.   The Donkey of Early, Mid and Late Spring

The woman holds on to the bed with hands and feet. The man stands behind her and embraces her waist with his hands. He then inserts the jade stalk into the jade gate. This is superlatively excellent.

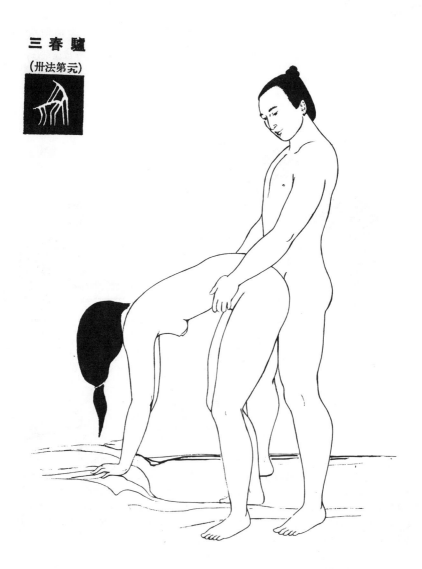

30. The Dog of Early, Mid-and Late Autumn

The man and woman are back to back, holding on to the mat with hands and feet. Their buttocks prop up one another. The male lowers his head, and with one hand he takes the jade thing and inserts it within the jade gate.[41]

三 秋 狗

（卅法第言）

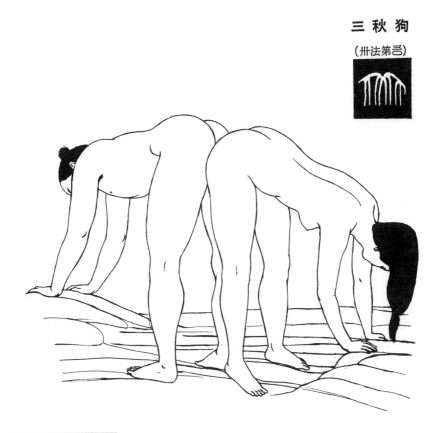

---

41. Perhaps ancient Chinese could perform intercourse in this posture because of the rearward location of the woman's vulva. R. T. Dickinson asserts that rearward location was a characteristic of primitive peoples and even Orientals (*Human Sex Anatomy*, Baltimore, 1933, 42), but van Gulik concludes that location of the vulva rearwards was an individual, rather than a racial, trait (*op. cit.*, p. 274).

CHAPTER XIV

Introduction

After having explained thirty positions of coitus, the Master of the Cave Profound observes that there are nine variations, depending on the slowness or quickness of the action, the direction, and the rhythm. His thesis forms a logical progreesion, from stating the principles behind the positions to showing the actions that man and woman should institute after uniting. These movements within coitus are intended to apply to all positions; therefore, the total number of conceivable types of intercourse, combining position and movement, amount to almost three hundred. The styles are effectively depicted through a series of vivid similes, with the motions of the jade stalk and the reactions of the jade gate likened to a series of phenomena observable in nature.

The Nine Styles

The Master of the Cave Profound said: " Generally the jade stalk strikes left or right like a fierce general crashing through the battle lines. This is its first style. It may rely on what is above or leap below, like a wild horse leaping into a mountain current. This is its second style. It may appear or disappear, like a flock of seagulls on the waves. This is its third style. It may build deeply or open shallowly, like a sparrow pecking at crow eaves. This is its fourth style. It may charge deeply or stab shallowly, like a great rock tossed into the sea. This is its fifth style. It may stir gently or push slowly, like a frozen snake entering a cave. This is its sixth style. It may strike quickly or stab suddenly, like a frightened mouse passing through a hole. This is its seventh style. It may lift up its head or detain its feet, like a hawk seizing a crafty hare. This is its eighth style. It may rise above or bow below, like a large sail encountering a wild wind. This is its ninth style."

CHAPTER XV

Introduction

The six postures analyze rhythm and action within coitus as follows:

1. A movement likened to a thrust between the shells of an oyster. It is forced open and the pearl is taken. This passage tells the man what to do when the sphincter muscles of the vagina are tense.

2. Action in which a strong rock is broken open with a chisel, and the jewel is removed from the rock. This imparts a definite rhythm to the portal in its deepest part.

3. Action of inserting a medical substance into the mortar and beating it with an iron pestle. This makes a strong and loosening impact on the portal.

4. A blacksmith, to forge iron, having the iron beaten first by four men who time their actions to one another's movements. By doing this, the iron ingots are gradually refined, even as they move from left to right above the metal bed beaten by the hammers. This is a simile for the vigorous timing of the insertion of the penis.

5. A peasant harvesting rice plants. The simile of a rice-polishing peasant suggests the rhythmic rubbing action that the penis should initiate.

6. The confrontation of two great cliffs that have been freshly cut. The position of man and woman side by side is comparable. The Dark Garden and the Heavenly Court adhere to one another like pulsating veins, with one motion indivisible for each.

The " six postures " thus represent somewhat exaggerated descriptions of the moves that take place from the beginnings of coitus to the achievement of orgasm.

The Six Postures

The Master of the Cave Profound said: " Generally, in intercourse one may press the jade stalk downwards and in going and coming slice at the jade veins.[21]   Its posture is like cutting open an oyster to take out the pearl. This is its first posture. Or below, it raises the jade veins, and above, charges the golden ditch; its posture is like slicing through rock in search of beautiful jade. This is its second posture. Or with the male tip it constructively charges the jade terrace.[20] Its posture is like an iron pestle striking a druggist's mortar; this is the third posture. Or it goes in and out with the jade stalk, attacking the examination hall left and right, like the refining of an iron hammered five times. This is its fourth posture. Or it goes back and forth with the male tip, rubbing and grinding between the god field and the forlorn valley,[23] like a peasant opening up the soil in autumn; this is its fifth posture. Or, through the Dark Garden and the Heavenly Court,[23] to grind and strike mutually; its posture is like the respective sounds of crumbling cliffs. This is its sixth posture."

CHAPTER XVI

Introduction

The next two chapters stress the efficacy of certain positions in sexual intercourse for curing many kinds of ailments. The passage reads like a medical prescription in which the penis is the curative agent, for the number and manner of its insertions are specifically prescribed. If the instructions are followed to the letter, the text states that in ten or twenty days a cure will be effected. One position enables the man to hold fast to his semen and checks undue loss of blood by the woman; another harmonizes the man's life-force and cures coldness in the woman's vagina. The magic number for penetrations is usually nine, an odd number associated with the male element and the number of greatest potency under ten. " Sex by the numbers " supplies further benefits to the practitioner; it strengthens the bones, profits the veins, enhances the fluids, invigorates the male, and cures odoriferousness of the vagina. To practice sex as advised, however, would be impractical for anyone gainfully employed. A typical instruction is to carry out intercourse in the prescribed way nine times daily for nine days, another indication that the text was compiled primarily for members of the leisure class. The nine times nine prescription represents the ultimate in male-oriented numerology.

The Eight Benefits

The Secrets of the Jade Bedroom states that the Woman Plain said: " Male-femalism has seven ills and eight benefits. The first benefit is called ' firming up the semen.' Have the woman lie on her side with thighs spread. The man lies between them on his side, carrying out a count of double nine. When the count is completed, he stops. (This) causes the male to firm up the semen, Also, to cure blood leakage of the woman, if (this is) carried out twice daily, (she) will be cured in fifteen days.

固　精

(八益第一)

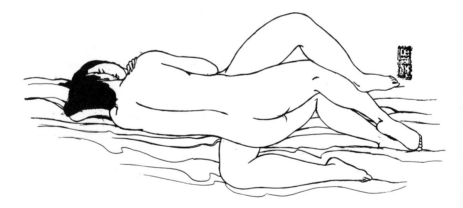

" The second benefit is called ' tranquilizing the life-force.' Have the woman lie straight out, pillow elevated and thighs spread. The male kneels between her thighs and stabs her, carrying out a count of triple nine. When the count ends, he stops. This causes the man's life-force to be harmonized. Also, to cure coldness in the woman's (jade) gate, if (this is) carried out three times daily, she'll be cured in twenty days.

安 気

(八益第二)

"The third benefit is called 'profitably hoarding.'" Have the woman lie on her side, bending both thighs. The man lies crosswise and then stabs her, carrying out a count of four nines and stopping when the count is completed. It causes the person's life-force to be harmonized; further, to cure a coolness of the woman's gate, if (this is) done four times daily, she'll be cured in twenty days.

利　蔵

（八益第三）

" The fourth benefit is called ' strengthening the bones.' Have the woman lie on her side, bending her left knee and extending her right thigh. The man kneels and stabs her, carrying out a count of five nines and stopping when the count is completed. It causes the man to blend the articulation of his joints. Further, to cure an obstruction of the woman's blood, if (this is) done five times daily, she'll be cured in ten days.

強　骨

（八益第四）

"The fifth benefit is called 'blending the conduits.' Have the woman lie on her side, bending her right leg and extending her left thigh. The man holds on to the ground and stabs her, carrying out a count of six nines and stopping when the count is completed. It causes the man's veins to profit throughout. Further, to cure excessive contraction of the woman's vagina, if (this is) done six times daily, she'll be cured in twenty days.

調　脈

（八益第五）

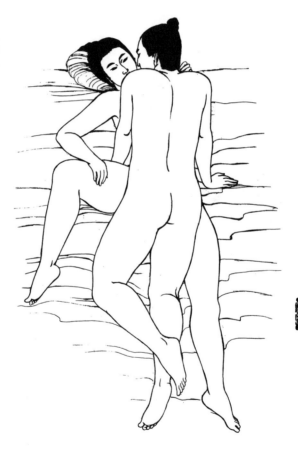

"The sixth benefit is called 'storing the blood.' The man lies down straight and has the woman transport her buttocks and kneel on top of him. He inserts the jade stalk extremely (deeply). Have the woman carry out a count of seven nines and stop when the count is completed. It causes a man's vigor to be strengthened. Further, to cure inefficacy of the woman's menstrual cycle, if (this is) done seven times daily, she'll be cured in ten days.

蓄　血

（八益第六）

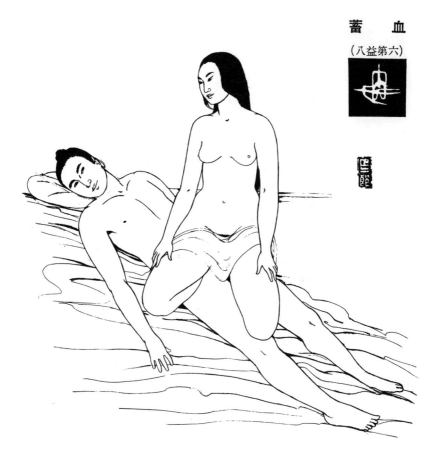

" The seventh benefit is called ' profiting the fluid.'   Have the woman
lie straight, face downwards, with her rear elevated.   The man mounts
her, carries out a count of eight nines and stops when the count is completed.   It causes the man's bones to be augmented.

益　液

(八益第七)

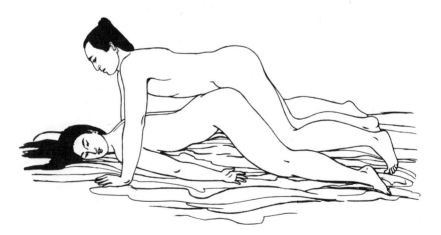

" The eighth benefit is called ' informing the body.' Have the woman lie straight out, bending her thighs and forcing her legs under her buttocks. The man makes use of his thighs and ribs and (then) stabs her. He thereby carries out a count of nine nines and stops when the count is completed. It causes the man's bones to be fulfilled. Further, to cure an odoriferousness of the woman's vagina, if (this is) done nine times daily, she'll be cured in nine days.

八益撮要 玉房秘決云	一益曰固精	二益曰安氣	三益曰利藏	四益曰強骨	五益曰調脉	六益曰畜血	七益曰益液	八益曰道體
状	女 側臥張股 男 側臥其中	女 正臥高枕伸張而肶 男 呿股間刺之	女 側臥屈兩股 男 橫臥卻刺之	女 側臥屈右膝伸左膝 男 伏刺之	女 側臥屈尻左膝伸右膝 男 振地刺之	女 戴尻跪男上極內之	女 正伏舉後 男 上往	女 正臥屈肶足追尻下 男 以胅脊刺之
効	治漏血 令固精	治井門寒 令人氣和	二益同	治用血 令關節調和	治廿門辟 令脈通利	治月經不利 令人力強	經文闕之 令人骨填	治陰裏 令人骨實
数	二九	三九	四九	五九	六九	七九	八九	九九
行	再行	三行	四行	五行	六行	七行	欬八行	九行
日	十五日	廿日	廿日	十日	廿日	十日	經文闕之	九日

(The "Eight Benefits" in Outline Form)

CHAPTER XVII

Introduction

This chapter deals exclusively with the techniques to be used when the man's body balance is out of harmony, the object being to relieve the various ailments that arise as a direct consequence of forced intercourse. Like advising someone who has a hangover to take a drink the next morning, the advice here to the man who has gotten sick through sexual indulgence is to indulge in more of the same. However, in these instances the man is ordered to assume a passive role; in no event is he to discharge semen. The first of the seven ills, "stopped air," prevents the man from having an erection and causes a decline in his life powers. He feels exhausted and is easily fatigued. This debility results from bedroom excesses and is caused by too much emission. The curative position is one in which the woman takes the initiative, and it is to be done nine times daily for ten days! The second of the seven ills, "semen overflow," contrasts with "stopped air" in being a physical, rather than a mental, affliction. It is caused by premature ejaculation and by engaging in coitus when drunk. Shallow penetrations of the penis constitute the cure. The Taoists believed that you should avoid sex when drunk or after a heavy meal; one of the causes of the third ill, "discordant veins," is in having intercourse before throughly digesting your food. Special consideration is again given to body position. The fourth ill, "life-force leakage," consists of fatigue through undue toil of the muscles. If one has coitus while still perspiring, the internal organs get out of harmony. The man's lips are dry, and the inside of his mouth feels rough. The cure is for the woman to mount the man with her back to him, in a position sometimes called "rear turret." The fifth ill, a chronic disease of the internal organs, causes the patient to expend considerable energy even to urinate and defacate. Coitus in such an instance can be disastrous, for the man thus aggravates his fatigue and induces impotence.   To effect a cure, the woman mounts the man, face to face, and is directed not to move.   Perhaps she is told to be inactive because the man is so extremely debilitated that he cannot endure too strong a stimulus.   Excessive intercourse leads to the sixth ill, that of "the hundred stoppages."   The man has exhausted his semen supply, and to replenish it the woman mounts him and assumes the initiative, giving of her essence while he holds back his semen and resupplies its source.   The last of the seven ills is "blood exhaustion," caused by continuous and deep coitus.   It destroys the vitality of the skin and injures the man's sexual organs.   The cure for this problem, caused by deep coitus with emission, is to practice deep coitus nine times daily for ten days, but without emission.   In conclusion, please note that the number *seven* of the "seven ills" belongs within the male category of odd numbers, next in efficacy to the number nine.

The Seven Ills

The Secrets of the Jade Bedroom states that the Woman Plain said: "The first ill is called 'stopped air.'   One whose air is stopped lacks desire in his heart but forces it.   Then perspiration flows and energy is cut off, causing his heart to heat up and his eyes to darken.   The way to cure this is to have the woman lie straight out.   The man supports both her thighs, deeply presses down with the jade stalk, and makes the woman agitate it herself.   When the woman's essence appears, he stops.   The man is not to continue until he attains joyfulness.   If (this is) practiced nine times daily, in ten days he'll be cured.

絶　気

（七損第一）

" The second ill is called ' semen overflow.' One whose semen overflows greedily enjoys this. He uses it before the female and male elements have harmonized, and halfway along his semen overflows. Furthermore, if he has intercourse when he's drunk and his breath vapors are chaotic, he harms his lungs. This causes the man to have a perverse upper breath and to become diabetic. He may be happy or angry, sad or cruel; his mouth is dry and his body hot, and it is hard for him to stand for a long while. The way to cure this is to have the woman lie down straight with both knees bent, scissored between the man. The man makes a shallow stab, inserting the jade stalk and making the woman agitate it herself. When the woman's essence appears, he stops. The man is not to continue until he attains joyfulness. If (this is) practiced nine times daily, in ten days he'll be cured.

溢　精

（七損第二）

" The third ill is called ' circulation out of order.' One with circulation out of order forcibly uses it when the female element is not firm. Halfway along, he forcibly leaks semen and his life-force is exhausted. After eating a full meal, he has intercourse and injures his spleen. It causes the man's food to be indigestible; his penis is impotent and he lacks semen. The way to cure this is to have the woman lie straight out, hooking the man's buttocks with her legs. The man then holds to the mat and inserts the jade stalk, making the woman agitate it herself. When the woman's essence appears, he stops. He is not to continue until he attains joyfulness. If (this is) practiced nine times daily, in ten days he'll be cured.

" The fourth ill is called ' energy leakage.' One who has energy leakage is exhausted; his perspiration comes out, and it won't dry up. And having intercourse causes his stomach to heat up and his lips to be scorched. The way to cure this is to have the man lie down, directly stretched out, with the woman sitting over him, legs astride, facing his feet. The woman holds to the mat and shallowly inserts the jade stalk. Have her agitate it herself. When her essence appears, stop. The man is not to continue until he attains joyfulness. If (this is) practiced nine times daily, he'll be cured in ten days.

気　泄

（七損第四）

"The fifth ill is called 'organs out of sequence.' Organs out of sequence mean injury to (the organs); one with this (ailment) suddenly has to urinate and defacate anew. If he forcibly applies the jade stalk when his body is not yet settled, he injures his liver. When he finally explodes in intercourse, his (rate) of slowness and quickness is unregulated; being unregulated, it wearies his sinews and bones. This causes his sight to become dimmed; ulcers and abcesses both arise, and all of his veins are withered and severed. After a long while, this gives rise to a partial withering away; the penis becomes impotent and will not arise. The way to cure this is to have the man lie straight out with the woman bestride his thighs. Squatting before him, she slowly and deliberately takes the lead and inserts the jade stalk. Don't let the woman agitate herself. When the woman's essence appears, stop. The man is not to continue until he attains joyfulness. If (this is) practiced nine times daily, in ten days he'll be cured.

機　関

(七損第五)

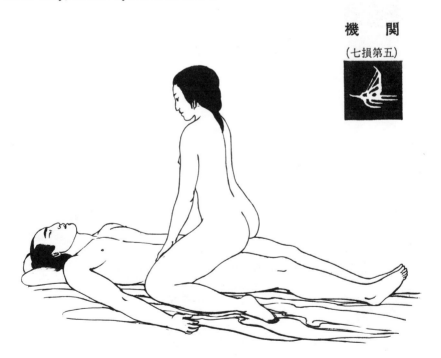

"The sixth ill is called 'the hundred stoppages.' One with the hundred stoppages is lewdly indulgent towards women, and he applies himself without restraint. He has intercourse frequently, loses (a sense of) proportion, and exhausts his semen. He forces himself and compels an emission, but the semen won't all come out. A hundred illnesses arise, and he becomes diabetic and his sight is dimmed. The way to cure this is to have the man lie straight out; the woman, bestride him on top, kneels forwards and holds on to the mat. Have the woman insert the jade stalk and agitate it herself. When her essence comes forth, stop. The man is not to continue until he attains joyfulness. If (this is) practiced nine times daily, in ten days he'll be cured.

百　閉

(七損第六)

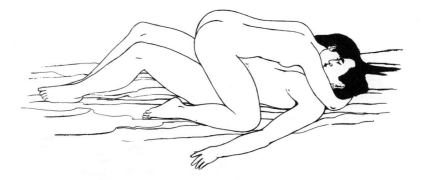

"The seventh ill is called 'blood exhaustion.' Those with blood exhaustion do things with effort, walk rapidly, and are fatigued, and they have intercourse while covered with perspiration. When they lie down, they forcefully push, submerging their original (force) and (becoming) suddenly explosive. Illnesses thereby arrive one after the other and can't be stopped. The blood dries up and the life-force is exhausted. It makes a man's skin weak and his flesh irritable. The (jade) stalk hurts, the bag (of the scrotum) is damp, and the semen changes into blood. The way to cure this is to have the woman lie straight out, raising her buttocks high and extending both thighs. The man kneels between (her thighs) and stabs deeply. He makes the woman agitate the jade stalk herself, stopping when her essence comes forth. The man is not to continue until he attains joyfulness. If (this is) practiced nine times daily, in ten days he'll be completely cured."

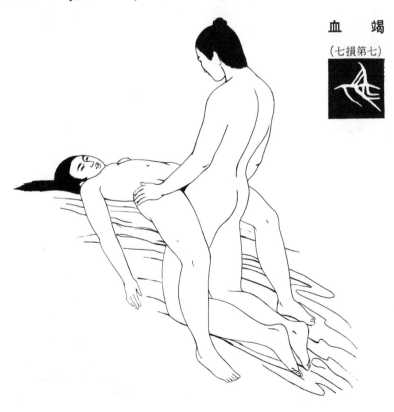

血　竭

（七損第七）

CHAPTER XVIII

Introduction

Ancient Chinese doctors regarded the movements of life phenomena as air and the latent quality of air in borrowed form as blood. Blood and semen were thought to transform the true essence of these phenomena into a oneness; thus, by the man's not leaking semen, it was converted into energy. To achieve longevity, a method was devised of " returning the semen," for it was believed that leakage of the semen removed the air and blood and hastened the aging process. In this chapter, the man is cautioned against quick leakage and is advised to extend the time for coitus, to ensure that he takes in the woman's emission. Having many contacts and changing women often are the points once again emphasized. To gain the objective of converting semen into life-energy by getting it to revert upwards to the brain, the man is advised to stop or interrupt coitus in order to prevent emission. Our Taoist text here implies a relationship between the reproductive glands and the internal secretions of the brain. The way to godliness for the devout Taoist male is through having emissionless coitus several dozen times a day— in other words, as often as he can.

Returning the Semen

The Secrets of the Jade Bedroom states that the Woman Selective said; " In intercourse, semen emission is regarded as pleasurable. Now if one closes it off and doesn't emit, what kind of pleasure can there be? " Replied P'eng the Methuselah: " When semen is emitted, the body is fatigued, the ears are pained and deafened with noise, and the eyes are pained and on the verge of sleep. The throat is completely dry and the joints are slackened. Though one is restored, it is but for a short while, and the joy ends in dissatisfaction. Now if one moves but doesn't emit, life-force and vigor are in excess, the body is well accomodated, and the ears and eyes are sharpened. While stressing quietude, you can again establish what you love in your heart. Since it is always insufficient (to quell your desire through emission), how can this (non-emission) be other than pleasurable?"

It further states that the Yellow Emperor said, "I wish to hear what the effect is like if you move but don't emit." Replied the Woman Plain: "If you move but don't emit, then your life-force and vigor are strengthened. If again you move but don't emit, your ears and eyes are sharpened. If a third time you move but don't emit, all sicknesses vanish. If a fourth time you move but don't emit, the five internal organs[42] are all pacified. If a fifth time you move but don't emit, the blood and veins are replete. If a sixth time you move but don't emit, the waist and back are hardened and strengthened. If a seventh time you move but don't emit, the buttocks and thighs are increasingly invigorated. If an eighth time you move but don't emit, the body begins to glow. If a ninth time you move but don't emit, longevity will not be lost. If a tenth time you move but don't emit, you can communicate with the gods."

The Essential Instructions of the Jade Bedroom states: "Those who can have intercourse several dozen times a day without losing their semen are cured of all ailments. Their longevity increases with each passing day. Further, if you often change the woman, the benefits increase as a consequence. Changing more than ten of them is best."

It further states that *The Classic of Immortals* said: "The way to return the semen and augment the brain is for one whose semen enlarges and in moving is about to come out to quickly take the two middle fingers of the left hand and press them behind the scrotum and in front of the big hole.[43] If this is done vigorously in exerting pressure, after exhaling long breaths and grinding the teeth several dozen times you won't shut off your energy. Then in bestowing the semen you can't get it to come forth. However, from the jade stalk it again returns upwards and enters the brain. This method has been transmitted by the Immortals, who

---

42. Namely, the liver, heart, spleen, lungs, and kidneys. (Cf. annotation in *Ishimpō*, p. 74.)
43. The anus.

all drank blood and made a pact that anyone who falsely transmitted it would later suffer calamity."

It further said; " If you wish to gain benefits while controlling a woman, but your semen is enlarged and moving, quickly raise your head, open your eyes wide, and look about left and right, above and below. (Further) tighten the lower part of your lower abdomen, close off your life energy, and the semen will naturally stop. Do not transmit this falsely. Those who can emit semen twice monthly or twenty-four times yearly all get to live one or two hundred years, with fine complexions and no ailments."

The Recipes of Priceless Gold states: " Formerly, at the start of the era of Virtuous Regard (ca. 627), there was an old rustic about seventy-old years of age who paid a call on me and said: ' Recently, for several tens of days my sex has been flourishing more and more. I think of carrying out the spring (-like) thing day and night with my wife, can accomplish it all, and am unaware that I am aged. Is this beneficial or bad for me?' I replied, saying: ' This is greatly inauspicious. Have you alone not heard of the burning of the fat? When the fat is about to be burned completely away, it always first darkens and then lightens. When the light ends, it is annihilated. Now your years are pressing those of the dying rays of the sun on the trees, and you have probably used your semen for a long while. How can your sudden ferocious arousal of spring feelings not transgress the Norm? I am worried about this for you. Will you make an effort? Forty days later you will get sick and die, the effect of not being cautious here.' Therefore, when one who is skilled in nourishing life realizes that his sex is flourishing, he is always careful to repress it. One cannot do as one pleases and exhaust one's intent so as to injure oneself. If you are able (even) once to restrain yourself and not leak, then that once you greatly increase the oil (of the human fat). If you cannot restrain yourself but give in to your feelings and emit, then when the fat of the fire is about to be annihilated you are removing the oil. One must guard deeply against this."

CHAPTER XIX

Introduction

The title of this chapter refers to ejaculation. The writer records the number of emissions that a man can have, dependent on age and physical condition. The Taoist practitioner of the bedroom arts is extremely fearful that the life-force may be exhausted, and so he cautions against semen wastage. But the writer in this instance believes that if one doesn't emit at all, the power of regeneration may be lost through alienation from the principles of sex and life. In ancient China, human actions were thought to correspond to the four seasons, with an unending cycle of birth, growth, accumulation, and storage. This was the sequence of the four seasons; to act contrary to it was to injure life. In spring, when the male element was in full force, it was permissible to emit frequently, but in winter, when the female element abounded, emission had to be severely restricted. Our text cites one passage from *The Recipes of Priceless Gold*.[44] Another passage in this work asserts that man should have coitus with woman twice monthly—in other words, twenty-four times a year. The text claims that those who do this live to be two hundred, with youthful complexions and no illnesses, and that they have only to supplement coitus with the proper medicines in order to live forever.[45]

Ejaculation and Leakage

The Secrets of the Jade Bedroom states that the Yellow Emperor asked the Woman Plain, " The essential of the Way is to wish not to lose

---

44. For the exact citation, see *The Recipes of Priceless Gold* 千金方, chapter 27.
45. *Ibid.*

semen; one should be sparing of the fluid. If one seeks a child, how should he obtain leakage?" Replied the Woman Plain; "There are men strong and weak, old and in their prime. Each should (live in) accord with his life-force vigor and not try to force joyfulness. Forcing joyfulness is injurious. Therefore, a flourishing male of fifteen can ejaculate twice daily; an emaciated one can ejaculate once daily.[46] A twenty-year-old can ejaculate twice daily, but once daily if he's thin. A thirty-year-old can emit once a day, or once every two days if he's an inferior specimen. One who is forty and flourishing emits once every three days, or once every four days if he's weak. One flourishing at fifty can emit once in five days, or if he's weak once in ten days. One who flourishes at sixty emits once in ten days, or once in twenty days if he's weak. One flourishing at seventy can emit once every thirty days or, if he's weak, not have any leakage."

The Compilation of the Essentials of Nourishing Life states that the Taoist Liu Ching[47] said: "You should emit semen once every three days in spring and twice monthly in summer and autumn. In winter, semen should be shut off. Now the Way of Heaven is to hoard the male element in winter. Man should pattern himself after this; he thereby gains a long life. One emission in winter is equal to a hundred in spring."

The Recipes of Priceless Gold states: "The Way of the Woman Plain is that men who are twenty leak once every four days; men who are thirty leak once every eight days; men who are forty leak once every sixteen days; men who are fifty leak once every twenty-one days. Men who are sixty completely close off their semen and do not leak again. If one's body strength is still vigorous, he is to leak once a month.

---

46. Classical texts dating back to the Han state that girls began to menstruate at fourteen and that boys started to emit sperm at sixteen. (Cf. van Gulik, *op. cit.*, 16.)

47. Liu Ching was a Taoist of Han times. He was said to have taken a medical concoction composed of mica for over 130 years, as a result of which he looked only thirty. He could foretell the future and get Heaven to prolong human lives. He supposedly was still actively instructing his disciples in the medical arts during the reign of the Martial Emperor of the Wei Dynasty 魏武帝; if so, he would have been more than 300 years of age. (*Ishimpō*, 56–57 n.)

There are some men whose life-force vigor is strong and flourishing. Those who exceed ordinary men can't repress and endure this; in not leaking for a long time, they get to be ulcerated.   If a man is past sixty, he should not have intercourse for fifty or sixty days.   If the desire for intercourse rises up irregularly in his mind, he should close off his semen and not leak."

The Master of the Cave Profound[48] says: " When one is about to leak semen, he must await the joyfulness of the woman and leak at the same time that she does.   The man should pull out shallowly, playing between the lute strings[27] and the wheat buds.[37]   The depths and shallows of the male tip are like an infant holding the breast in its mouth.   In other words, closing one's eyes and internalizing one's thoughts, the tongue supports the lower palate; one crooks the back, stretches the head, dilates the nose, contracts the shoulders, closes the mouth, and takes (deep) breaths—then the semen naturally ascends.   The degree of restraint is alwys dependent (on this); out of ten such times, one can only leak twice or thrice."

---

48.   van Gulik, *op. cit.*, 123, cites an allegation by Maspero that this might have been a reference to Li Tung-hsüan, a seventh-century Chinese scholar and physician.   However, Dr. Ishihara's studies reveal that the person quoted here was the T'ang Taoist leader Chang Ting 張鼎, who used the appelation *Tung-hsüan-tzu* 洞玄子 for the works he wrote on the bedroom arts.   (See *Ishimpō*, 38–39n.)

CHAPTER XX

Introduction

This chapter considers cures for the decline of a man's vigor when he has abused the bedroom arts. It cautions in general against sudden and violent boudoir behavior and advocates cultivation of the life-force and the accumulation of semen. The nature of the semen discharge tells the specialist which organ is diseased. Having intercourse in improper positions or at improper times leads to a host of affllictions; these are mentioned, and the remedies are given. The emphasis here is on having intercourse after midnight and as dawn approaches; during coitus, one is advised to be leisurely in movement and to adjust one's breathing accordingly. Taoist gymnastics and breathing exercises are also prescribed as ways to strengthen the eyes, ears, and digestive organs and the waist and back muscles; these exercises also have curative value. Apart from conferring these side benfits, the main purpose of Taoist bedroom techniques is to assure return of the semen.

Curing Illnesses

The Secrets of the Jade Bedroom states that the Master of Primordial Harmony said: " Now indulging in extreme feelings as one wishes inevitably conveys (with it) serious illness. This is something made evident through the experience of intercourse. Since one gets sick in this way, one can also get cured in this way. It is sufficient to note the simile of sobering up through (drinking) wine."

It further states that the Woman Selective asked, " What signs are there of man's flourish and decline? " Replied P'eng the Methuselah: " If the male element flourishes and secures the life-force, then the jade stalk should be hot[49] and the semen should be thick and congealed. There are five (signs) of its decline:

" The first is called ' the appearance of the semen through leakage '; this is an injury to vitality.

" The second is called ' semen clear and scarce '; this is an injury of the flesh.

" The third is called ' the semen changes and smells '; this is an injury of the muscles.

" The fourth is called ' the semen comes out but is not shot forth '; this is an injury of the bones.

" The fifth is called ' the penis deteriorates and doesn't arise '; this is an injury of the body.

"These injuries are all caused from not having intercourse gently but from having sudden emissions instead. The method of cure is to control (the woman) and not emit. Within a hundred days, your life-force vigor will invariably increase a hundredfold."

It further says: " In having intercourse, if you open the eyes to look at one another's bodies and at night if you light a fire and read books, you will have a sickness of obscure vision and blindness. The method of cure is to have intercourse at night with the eyes closed.

" In having intercourse, those who, in taking the enemy, ride on their bellies and those who respond to this from below by raising their waists are distressed by waist pains as a consequence. Urgency (is felt) in the abdomen, both legs are cramped, and the back is bent. The method of cure is to insert, straighten the body, and play leisurely.

" If in having intercourse one lies down sideways, facing the enemy, and raises the enemy's buttocks in his hands, he is afflicted with pain in the ribs. The way to cure this is to lie down straight and play leisurely.

" If, in having intercourse, you lower your head and extend your neck, you'll be afflicted by the illness of a heavy head and a stiff neck. The way to cure this is to place your head on top of the enemy's brow without lowering it.

" If you have intercourse when you've eaten too much, called ' playing at midnight when your food is not yet digested,' you'll be afflicted by

---

49. The fact that the semen was hot implied good body circulation.

sores. The chest is full of vapors; there seems to be a pulling below the ribs and a rending within the chest. You lose desire for food and drink, obstructions accumulate in the stomach, and from time to time you vomit green and yellow (matter).[50] The stomach, too, is full of vapors and the veins contract. You may disgorge blood from the nose, have hard pains below the ribs, and develop ugly sores on your face. The way to cure this is to have intercourse past midnight and near the dawn.

" Having intercourse when you've drunk too much is called ' being drunk in intercourse.' You use up your energies in play and, in deep extremity, are afflicted with illnesses of yellow and black ulcers. There is pain below the ribs and a drawing in of your breath. When you move your hands, there is a feeling in the buttocks below as if the scrotum were filled with water. There is a loosening above the navel and shoulders and the wrists (feel) drawn. In extreme cases, chest and back hurt, you cough blood, and suffer from dizziness. The way to cure this is never again to drink hot wine[51] and to have intercourse towards dawn, playfully and leisurely relaxing your body.

" If you don't urinate when you should but have intercourse instead, you'll be afflicted with an illness in which your urine drips. The abdominal vapors expand, urination is difficult, and there is an aching pain within the (jade) stalk. One is always wanting to take it into one's hands, and on (one's) doing so, (urine) drips out. The way to cure this is to first urinate and then lie down and settle yourself. If you have intercourse leisurely a short while later, you'll be cured.

" If you need to defacate but don't, and have intercourse instead, you will be afflicted with hemorrhoids. The feces are hard to eliminate and are diarrhetic. In time, bloody pus descends and anal fistulas arise, which look like bee holes. When you lean on the toilet,[52] feces

---

50. Green referred to the color of water from the gall bladder; yellow, to water in the stomach.

51. The Chinese custom of drinking wine hot can be traced back more than three thousand years, to the Shang dynasty. The Shang people used a tripod-shaped goblet for this purpose, heating it and drinking two types of wine.

52. The ancient Chinese " toilet " was primarily in the form of iron buckets, one for urination and another for defecation. These are still used in Japan on occasion by young children and by old people. Here the reference in our text is probably to an outhouse situated along the banks of a river, like the *kawaya* in Japanese.

come out irregularly and growths ache painfully—you lie down but can't rest. To cure this through the Way, rise at cockcrow and go to the toilet. Lie down again and settle yourself. Then if you play together leisurely, perfecting your body and delaying your intent, causing her to become slippery smooth and then withdrawing (your penis), the sickness will be cured and (you'll feel) godly. The woman's ailment likewise will be cured.

"If you exceed moderation in intercourse, you'll have a beadlike perspiration. Elastic and turning aside, wind arises and is carried within; the semen is empty, and the life-force is exhausted. When cold enters the body, one is sickened, weakened and lamed, and the hands can't be raised to the head. The way to cure this is to nourish your spirit attentively and drink a boiled prescription called Earth Yellow."[53]

It further states that Shaman Tzu-tu said: "The way to cause a man's eyes to be clear is (as follows): When you are moved and about to emit, you should raise your head, shut off your breath, and (then) take a great breath. Glaring and looking left and right you tighten your stomach and return the semen vapors, causing them to enter your veins.

"The way to cause yourself not to become deaf is (as follows): When on the verge of emitting fluid, you should swallow your breath greatly, grind your teeth, shut off energy, and cause a wind-soughing sound within your ears. You should further tighten the stomach, breathe regularly, and diffuse it to a firmness. Then till old age you won't become deaf.

"The way to regulate the five viscera,[42] digest food, and cure the hundred ailments is (as follows): Approaching emission, extend your stomach and through your will absorb the outside ethers. If you then shrink (your stomach), the semen is later scattered and it returns to the myriad veins. If you go between the lute strings[27] and the wheat buds[37] with nine shallows and one deep, the health-giving vapors return, and the vapors of illness scatter and leave. The way to cause a man's back to be without pain is to have him press his waist against a wall and make it level (with it), without raising or lowering it to extremes. Then when he practices (intercourse) he'll always cause (the woman) to flow. If he wishes to prevent weaknesses, nourish the body and cure illness,

---

53. The Chinese medicine, literally called "Earth Yellow," was made up of foxglove in either a dried or raw state. (See Index of Medical Terms.)

when he's about to emit he should not. The semen flows back centrally, and in the midst of the flow passes through heat."

It further says: "Now the Way of the female and male elements is to treasure the emission fluid. If you take loving care of it, life can be preserved. In general, after emission you should take the woman's life-force to augment your own. Also, in establishing (the count of) nine, keep to the nine (count) and (then) rest. If you wish to avoid (emitting even) once, press with the left and right hands hard below the perineum and the semen will be returned and the fluid restored. The taking of the life-force is (through) nine shallows and one deep. (The man) touches his adversary's mouth with his own and breathes through the mouth. (The woman) draws in her feminine breaths and (the man) doesn't swallow them. When he reaches her life-force, he suppresses (his agitation). When (his suppression) reaches the inner organs, this assists (the excitement of) the woman, and her energy thus becomes concentrated. Repeat it shallowly three times like this. The nine shallows and one deep (technique) being a nine (times) nine (equals) eighty-one (technique), it is full of male element numbers. When the jade stalk is hardened, it is taken out; weakened, it is inserted. This is called 'weakly entering and strongly leaving.' The harmonizing of the female and male element takes place between the lute strings[27] and the wheat buds.[37] The penis is (first) fixed beneath mixed rock,[28] and then it affixes itself (more deeply) among the wheat buds. If the penetration is shallow, it gets her essence; if it is (too) deep, her essence escapes. On getting to the grain seed,[25] you injure the liver. Your tears come forth on encountering a wind, and you drip an excess of urine. On getting to the odoriferous mouse, you injure your lungs, have coughing fits, and feel pain in your waist and back. On getting to the mixed rock, you injure your spleen. The stomach fills, and from time to time you have a foul-smelling diarrhea. Both thighs hurt, and a hundred ailments arise in the mixed rock, which therefore harms intercourse. When you unite, don't wish to unite what is distant."

The Yellow Emperor asked, "If one violates these prohibitions, what can be done for a cure?" Replied Tzu-tu: "You should be restored and cured through women. The way is to have the woman lie straight out with her thighs spread apart nine inches.[54] The man goes

---

54. See note 26.

forth in accord with this, and first drinks the jade fluid.[55]   After a long while he then plays with the vast stream.[56]   He inserts the jade stalk leisurely, restraining it with his hand.   Then, on arriving between the lute strings and the wheat buds, the enemy dances lewdly and is flustered at heart.   You should always maintain hardness but not have an emission.   Plan thirty breaths, cause the jade stalk to be hard and stong, and then insert it leisurely.   Let it get to the mixed rock, which should be at the height of a flood.   If it floods, take out (the penis) and rest a while.   The sickly and weak again insert it, always causing it to enter weak and to come out strong.   Before ten days have passed, it will be as strong as iron and as hot as fire, and in every battle it will be indefatigable."

---

55. The saliva.
56. Ostium urethrae externum.

CHAPTER XXI

Introduction

This chapter records the theory and methodology of conception, but most of it is related to taboos, and it has much the same content on taboos as the twenty-fourth chapter. It refers to days of ill omen in the T'ang calendar which are little understood today, stating that one should avoid intercourse on such days. Special attention is also paid to the waxing and waning phases of the moon. This was associated with the popular belief that life and death were influenced by the ebb and flow of the tide. One was advised to avoid having coitus on days of ill omen, since children born from such issue would be affected by the ill omen as well. It was best to have coitus after midnight. Having coitus on the first three odd-numbered male element days immediately after the cessation of menstruation produced a healthy, intelligent and long-lived boy, and having coitus on the first three even-numbered days after menstruation produced a girl. It was best not to have intercourse from the sixth day onwards. Ancient Taoist texts also warned against conceiving during times of natural or man-made calamities. The last night of the twelfth month was tabooed because on that night all the demons were out in force. It was considered ideal to conceive in the morning, especially before dawn, when the spirits of Heaven and Earth were calm and the life-force was ascendant. The death-force set in during the afternoon. According to ancient Chinese medical theory, women could conceive from age thirteen to forty-seven; men, from fourteen to fifty-five. Certain magic processes, such as eating small red beans at the time of intercourse, were said to ensure conception, and wine-drinking was considered by one source as a way to improve the quality of the child. An old man could conceive by having intercourse with a young woman, and a woman of fifty could do likewise through a young spouse.

Seeking Children

The Recipes of Priceless Gold states: "Now procreation through marriage is the fundament of human relations and the basis of the civilizing influences. When the sages set up their teachings, they explained the principles in detail, but their descendants were unable to understand these minutely, and they approached the event that day muddled and foolish. I shall now state in detail the way to seek a child, in order to hand this down to posterity. Like-minded gentlemen may perhaps look this over."

It further states: "Now those who wish children should first understand the fundamental destinies of husband and wife, the mutual begetting of the Five Elements, virtue, and union. Furthermore, the fundamental destiny does not reside in the non-conception of children, abolition of death, and grave (days of ill omen of the T'ang calendar). Therefore, those who seek and beget children will inevitably get them (if they avoid the above days of ill omen). If their fundamental destinies destroy and are destroyed by the Five Elements, if they collide with incrimination and death, and if (the days of conception) are on (the days of ill omen of) non-conception of children, abolition of death, and the grave, then the begetting of children cannot be sought. Be cautious and do not reflect (overmuch) on this. If you obtain a child later (nevertheless), you (may) wish to show it to others. If it is one mutually desired who is to receive blessings and virtue, (the intercourse) should be in accord with the rules. If you therefore avoid the taboos, the child that you bear will be utterly good and beautiful. It is hard to describe this in detail."

It also says: "Now those who wish to cause their children to be of good fortune should avoid the following days for intercourse: the fire days, the first and last quarter and the first and last days of the moon; times of great winds, storms, fogs, cold, and heat; when thunder and electricity resound, when heaven and earth are obscured, when there is no sunlight or moonlight; and during rainbows, earthquakes, and eclipses of the sun and moon. If there is conception at these times, not only does it increase a hundredfold the injury to the parents but the child that is born may be dumb, deaf, stupid and dull, insane, crooked and lamed, or blind. It will have many illnesses and be short-lived, neither filial nor humane. One should further avoid as not being permissible (having intercourse) under firelight and starlight, in chapels and temples, alongside wells, kitchens, and privies, and beside graves, corpses, and coffins."

It further states: " Now if intercourse is done according to the rules, there will be blessings and virtues. Great sages and men of goodness descended from the pregnant womb. Therefore, one should (cause) parents to be harmonious in their sex behavior and to respond mutually in what they do. The ways of the family (then) will flourish day by day, and omens of good fortune will compete with one another to assemble (first at the home). If you do not act in accordance with the rules, then there will be few blessings. Fools and evil ones will come into the womb and cause the sexual behavior of the parents to be hazardous. Whatever they do won't have (the desired) results, the ways of the family will be denied more with each passing day, and inauspicious omens will be frequent. Even though ones (thus) begotten grow up, they will be nation-destroyers and self-killers. Now the portents of blessings and disasters are in such influences. These, therefore, being the essential principles, how can one fail to reflect on them? "

It further says: " If after midnight at the time of the birth force you emit semen and have children, they will all be males, invariably long-lived, intelligent, and eminent." (Dr. Ishihara's note: According to *The Classic of the Great Purity*, midnight to noon constitutes the birth force and noon to midnight constitutes the death force.)

It further states, " The days of best omen are the days of royal visage and noble lodging." (Dr. Ishihara's note: These days are referred to in *The Classic of the Great Purity*.)

The Classic of Childbirth states that the Yellow Emperor said: "A person's first being born is based on a uniting of the female and male elements. Now when the female and male elements are united, one must avoid the nine portents. The nine portents are: First, a child born when the sun is on high will vomit up his food. Second, a child of midnight, when Heaven and Earth are barricaded, will be either dumb, deaf, or blind. Third, a child of the sun's eclipse will be distressed and injured in body. Fourth, a child of thunder and electricity, because of

Heaven's anger and ferocity, will easily become crazy. Fifth, a child of the moon's eclipse will commit evil with his mother. Sixth, a child of the rainbow will perform an ill-omened (deed) in his youth. Seventh, a child born during either the winter or summer solstices will injure its father and mother. Eighth, a child born during a crescent or full moon will inevitably initiate a troop rebellion and become blindly violent. Ninth, a child (conceived in) drunkenness or when gorged with food will inevitably be afflicted with madness, ulcers and hemorrhoids, and have sores."

It further states: "There are five things of ill omen to consider in begetting a child. The first consideration is when menstruation has not yet ceased. The second consideration is when the parents have boils. The third consideration is when the mourning garments have not yet been removed. The fourth consideration is when not yet cured from typhoid and when in personal mourning for your parents. The fifth consideration is when burdened personally by worries and fears and repeatedly startled and agitated."

The Secret Instructions of the Jade Bedroom states: "In the union of the female and male elements there are seven things to avoid. The first avoidance is a union of the female and male elements during the last or first day of the moon, when the moon is crescent or full. This injures the life-force, so that the child one begets will inevitably commit transgressions. One should be deeply cautious about this.

"The second avoidance is a union of the female and male elements when there are thunder, wind, and influences from Heaven and Earth. The blood and veins dance about, so that the child one begets will inevitably have ulcers and swellings.

"The third avoidance is a union of the female and male elements when one has just drunk wine, has gorged oneself with food, and hasn't yet digested these. There is a strong rumbling in the stomach, and the urine is a dirty white. Because of this, if you beget a child it will inevitably become insane.

"The fourth avoidance is a union of the female and male elements when you have newly urinated and the semen force is exhausted. Passage through the veins becomes obstructed. Because of this, if you beget a child it will inevitably die early.

"The fifth avoidance is a union of the female and male elements when you are fatigued and heavily burdened and have not yet tranquilized your spirit. The muscles and the waist ache painfully. Because of this, if you beget a child it will inevitably die early.

" The sixth avoidance is a union of the female and male elements when you have just bathed and your hair and skin are not yet dry. This causes a person's breath to become asthmatic. Because of this, if you beget a child it will inevitably be incomplete.

" The seventh avoidance is when (the penis) is war-strong and fully angered but harassed by pain in the passage (from urine accumulation?). If you then permit intercourse to take place, there is internal injury and sickness.

Such constitute the seven injuries."

It further says: " If a child is born deaf and dumb, it is of the last night of the last month (of the lunar calendar). That night all the demons meet, and they do not rest throughout the night. The gentleman abstains from sex, but the petty man secretly has intercourse, and his child invariably is deaf and dumb.

" If a child after birth becomes injured or dies, it is called the child of fire. If you light a lantern and have intercourse before the flame has gone out, if there is a child it will invariably die or be injured by the townspeople.

" If a child is born insane, it is one of thunder and lightning. During the great rains and rumblings of thunder in the fourth and fifth months, the gentleman abstains from sex, but the petty man secretly has intercourse. If there is a child, it will invariably be insane.

" If a child is born and eaten by a tiger or a wolf, it is one (born during) the serious observance of mourning (for one's parents). The filial son wears hempen clothes and abstains from eating meat. The gentleman is weakened and distressed, but the petty man secretly has intercourse. If there is a child, it will invariably be eaten by a tiger or a wolf.

" If a child is born and it dies of drowning, (it is because) its parents have transgressed. They conceal the placenta in a bronze vessel and bury it beneath a shaded wall, putting it seven feet into the ground. They call (the placenta) ' the young lad enclosed within,' and (the child) drowns in the water."

It further says: "A child (conceived during) a great wind will often be ill; a child conceived during thunder and lightning will be insane; a child conceived during a great drunkenness will invariably be madly extravagant; a child conceived during the menses will die in military service; a child conceived at twilight will undergo frequent changes; a child conceived when everyone is at rest will be either deaf or dumb; a child conceived during sunset will be ill-omened of mouth and tongue; a child conceived in the daytime will be afflicted by epilepsy; a child conceived in the afternoon will injure itself."

It further states that the Woman Plain said: "The way to seek a child is naturally unchanging. Purify the body, make the heart remote, tranquilize the thought, settle the dress, transmit an emptiness, and abstain. Three days after the woman's menstruation, past midnight and prior to cockcrow, play joyfully and cause the woman to be fully moved. Then go forward in accord with this, matching its doctrines and sharing its delights (with her). Withdraw your body, and in emitting don't go so far as to reach the wheat buds. If it is too far, then it passes by the child-door[57] and doesn't enter the womb. If you rely on the Taoist arts to have a child, it will be virtuous, good, and long-lived."

It further states that P'eng the Methuselah said: "The way to seek a child is truly to collect and nourish the semen force; you should not waste it frequently in emissions. When the woman's monthly (menstrual) event ends, she should cleanse and purify herself. If she has intercourse on the third and fifth days, the child she begets, if a boy, will be intelligent, talented, wise, long-lived and loftily eminent. If a girl, she will be pure and virtuous and shall wed a man of eminence."

It further states: "If you always control the female and male elements at the time approaching dawn, you benefit your body and improve your physique. The glory of your semen will be increasingly proclaimed. If a child is begotten, it will be rich and long-lived."

It further states that the Woman Plain said: "Now, everyone in having intercourse should shun what is prohibited. If he always avails himself of the force of life, there will be none who is not long-lived. If husband and wife grow old together, even though children are born they will not achieve longevity."

It further says: "If a man and a woman fulfill hundred-year life

---

57. The vagina.

spans, the children begotten will not be long-lived. If an eighty-year-old man can control a woman of fifteen to eighteen years of age, then children can be begotten. If the prohibitions are not transgressed, all of them will live to old age. If a woman of fifty gets a young spouse, she too can beget a child."[58]

It further states: "A pregnant woman, before the third month of pregnancy is completed, should remove the accessory[59] from a man's cap, burn it to ashes on the twenty-fifth day of the sexagenary cycle, put the ashes in rice wine, and drink them down. If she begets a child it will be rich, eminent, intelligent, and discerning. Keep this secret! Keep this secret!"

It further says: "If the woman is childless, have her hold in her left hand fourteen little red beans, while with her right hand she supports the tip of the man's penis and inserts it into her vagina. While touching the beans in her left hand with her mouth, she herself inserts the penis into the vagina. As she feels the semen coming down from the man's penis, she should eat the beans. There is full efficacy (in this), without a single failure."

The Master of the Cave Profound said: " In general, if you wish to seek children, wait till after the woman's menstruation has ended and have intercourse as follows: the first and third days after the end of menstruation will produce a boy; the fourth and fifth days, a girl. After the fifth day, one merely injures the strength of the emission, and in the end there are no benefits.

" When you have intercourse and emit semen, wait till the woman becomes joyful; you should leak together with her. And when you leak, you must do so completely. First have the woman lie straight out, heart stilled and intent uniform, eyes closed and thoughts internalized, receiving the life-force of the semen. Thereby, Lao-tzu said, ' The child you get at midnight will have greatest longevity, the child you get before midnight will have middle longevity, and the child you get

---

58. Western medical works posit 45 to 50 as the ages during which a woman usually ceases to menstruate, thereby ending the chance for further child-bearing.

59. The accessory to a man's cap, affixed behind his head, was colored so as to indicate his official status.

after midnight will have least longevity.' "[60]

It further says: "In general, after women have become pregnant they should do good things. They are not to look at evil colors or hear evil words; neither should they dwell upon their lewd desires. They are not to abuse or curse, get frightened, or fatigued, make wild statements, or worry. They are not to eat foods which are raw, cold, vinegary, smooth, or hot. They are not to ride in horse-drawn carriages, climb heights, look out over depths, descend slopes, make sudden movements, eat dumplings, or (be treated by) acupuncture.[61] They are always to be still at heart and correct in thought, listening always to the correct canon. This will finally cause the boys or girls they beget to be intelligent, wise, truthful, and good. This is the so-called instruction in the womb."

---

60. This quotation is not to be found in the *Tao-te-ching*. Perhaps it formed part of an edition no longer extant or referred to a different Taoist text.

61. Acupuncture was regarded as a special medical treatment, and it was feared that a pregnant woman would be adversely influenced by it. She was also advised to avoid taking strong medicines during pregnancy.

CHAPTER XXII

Introduction

Here the concept of woman is primarily physiological, as the writer gives his masculine views on what the attributes of a satisfactory bed partner should be. His insistence that she be complaisant and graceful echoes the words in a ninth-century T'ang manual about the properly-reared female, which likewise stressed that woman be yielding and obedient. But the Confucian description of womanhood emphasized the homemaking talents of the woman, who was expected to excel in sewing and in kitchen tasks and to stay in her quarters in blissful ignorance of the world beyond.[62] Our Taoist analyst is more interested in the good woman's being youthful, full bosomed, and amply fleshed, and he asserts that her figure should glow with health. Her joints must not protrude, but be well concealed in the flesh of her hands and feet. The ideal that he depicts seems to tally closely with the female models of corpulence that appear in paintings done towards the close of the T'ang. The Taoist hypothesizes that the best bed partner shakes in uncontrollable agitation, adjusts her movements to those of the man, and enriches him with an overflow of emission fluid. He states that one can't go wrong with a woman fitting the above description, for she invariably benefits the man and prolongs his years.

---

62. "A good wife was to leave the house as seldom as possible and to avoid gossip; if she did go out, she was advised to cover her face. . . . A model woman was virtuous, obedient, proper, harmonious, and yielding." (H. S. Levy, "T'ang Courtesans, Ladies and Concubines," in Orient/West, March, 1962, 61.)

(Sexually) Good Women

The Secrets of the Jade Bedroom states that Harmony Master Chung said: " Complaisance and grace constitute the beauty of the feminine nature. Now if (a woman) can attain to a perfect figure, rectifying shortcomings and joining in appropriate union, she'll not only please the heart and eye but, moreover, especially benefit her life and prolong her years.[63]

It further says: "If you wish to control women, you should secure youthful ones. They should not yet be full bosomed, but amply fleshed, with silken hair and small eyes. The whites and blacks of the eyeballs should be clearly defined,[64] face and figure glossy smooth, and words and voice harmonious. And below, the bones of each joint of the four limbs should be concealed in abundant flesh and not be too large. Hair below her vagina and ribs is undesirable; if there are (body hairs), they should be tiny and smooth."

The Text of Great Purity states that the Yellow Emperor asked, "What would you say about the woman who meets the standard?" Replied the Woman Plain: "The woman who meets the standard is naturally pleasant and accommodating; her voice is settled and her silken hair is black. She has delicate skin, slender limbs, and is neither tall or short, large or small. The slit between her thighs is high,[65] there is no hair on her pubic region, and her emission fluid is abundant. Her

---

63. The unwritten implication in this sentence is that she should control her desires.

64. This part of the description is also found in the ancient *Book of Odes;* it forms part of a formula description of woman which goes back to pre-Confucian days. (See citation in Legge, *The Chinese Classics*, Vol. IV, Part I, Prologomena, 144.) The ancient Chinese beauty was described through similies: fingers like blades of grass, skin like congealed ointment, a neck like the tree-grub, teeth like melon seeds, etc. (Cf. H. S. Levy, *A Feast of Mist and Flowers*, pp. 7–8.) In describing a woman, the Confucianists alluded to her beauty, while the Taoists revealed her anatomy.

65. See note 41.

years are from twenty-five to thirty,[66] and she has not yet given birth. During intercourse, her emission fluid overflows and her body moves and shakes. She can't control herself; perspiration flows in all directions, and she behaves in accord with the man. Even though the man doesn't practice the Way, if he gets this kind of woman he won't hurt himself."

It further states: " Slender limbs, delicate tissues, soft flesh, elegant texture, skin pure white and pale, finger joints slender and hollow, ears and eyes elevated, white complexioned, neither short nor tall. Thick thighs, a high slit, and a body compact throughout. Furthermore, she has no (body) hair, her body is as smooth as silk, and her pubic region is as soft as grease. If you practice the Way with this (kind of woman) you won't get tired all night, and as the husband you will be benefitted as a consequence. If you beget children, they will be noble and heroic."

It further says: " The way of appearance for men of distinction and women of eminence is to try to attain to smooth flesh and delicate limbs, to concentrate on being mild tempered; to have hair as lustrous as lacquer, pleasing and beautiful features, and no hair on the sex organs.[67] They should be fine voiced in speech, and the (angle of the) aperture (of the female vagina) should face frontwards. If you have intercourse with persons like these, you'll not be fatigued throughout the day. If you strive for women like these, you can thereby nourish your sex and prolong your years."

---

66. Many T'ang stories refer to a woman's beauty as first becoming noticeable at about thirteen or fourteen years of age. In Han and earlier times, the permissible marriageable age for a girl was usually considered as being between fourteen and twenty years of age. After twenty, the girl was regarded as having passed the appropriate time for marriage. (See *Chung-kuo fu-nü sheng-huo shih*, Commercial Press, Shanghai, 1937, 32–33.)

67. There is a modern Japanese saying which praises the beauty of a woman with skin fine and soft, no hair on the lower part of her body, and a lustrous head of hair.

CHAPTER XXIII

Introduction

This again is primarily a physiological description of an evil woman, except for the comment that she is high spirited, uncontrolled, and jealous. Jealousy was one of the cardinal sins in T'ang society, and many stories were circulated about enraged upper-class wives who opposed polygamy and made life miserable for their husbands' concubines. But again, the important things for the man to look for are strictly external: Does she, for example, have hair on her arms and shins and, if so, is it coarse? (Very little body hair and fine body hair seem to have been the Taoist ideals.) The hotness of the vagina was a prerequisite to beneficial sex, and the man was warned that a woman with a cold vagina would irrevocably harm him and that the damage from one encounter would be equal to that of a hundred. The masculine-type woman was greatly feared; she gave evidence of masculinity through her voice range, the prevalence of an Adam's apple, and the mannish configuration of her sex organs. One was also warned to stay away from women who were hard boned, over forty, red haired, pockmarked, or emaciated. The statement about "lewd liquids" probably refers to the woman who ejaculated prematurely and had an odoriferous discharge.

(Sexually) Evil Women

The Secrets of the Jade Bedroom states: "The appearance of the evil woman is somewhat as follows: disheveled hair, pockmarked face, mallet neck, Adam's apple, dark teeth, gruff voice, large mouth, high nose, muddied eye pupils, long hair on mouth and chin, and seeming to have a beard. Her bones and joints are prominent and large, she is yellow haired and skimpily fleshed, and the hairs on her pubic region are large and strong, and in most cases they grow inversely. If you have intercourse with her she will harm you every time."

It further says: "The woman's skin is uncontrollably coarse, her body is uncontrollably emaciated, and her constant accord with the high and affixing to the low likewise can't be controlled. She has a man's voice and is high spirited and uncontrolled; likewise uncontrolled are the hairs on her thighs and shins. Uncontrollable too are her jealousy, the coldness of her pubic region, her inauspicious overhastiness, her overgorging on foods, and the fact that she is over forty years old. Neither can she control the unsettled state of her inner organs or the inversion of her hairs. Her body is always uncontrollably cold and her bones uncontrollably hard; she is uncontrollably curly haired and has an Adam's apple; she is ill smelling at the armpits and produces lewd liquids.

The Text of Great Purity states that the way to appraise a woman is to inspect closely the hair below her pubic region and under her armpits. One should cause her to be pliant and slippery smooth. But on the contrary if she is perverse above, has hair on her arms, and is coarse and unsmooth, intercourse with such a woman will harm the man every time. Though you unite with her but once, it will have the same effect as uniting with her a hundred times.

It further says: "If the woman's sex organ is masculine shaped, accords with the waxing and waning of the moon, and is an organ of virility, intercourse will damage the man most severely. If she is red haired, pockmarked, emaciated, sickly, and dispirited, intercourse with her is of no benefit to the male."

CHAPTER XXIV

Introduction

This chapter refers to various taboos observed in connection with coitus, and is similar in content to the twenty-first chapter on seeking children.   But in contrast to the earlier chapter, which emphasizes conception and pregnancy, taboos are viewed here within a larger context.   Here too we see a heavy admixture of Taoist superstitions based on the philosophy of the male-female elements and get some idea of the fetters of ignorance which dictated aspects of aristocratic life in the Sui, T'ang, and Heian periods.   No important new information about Chinese medical and sex practices is given, but there is much here of potential interest to the folklorist.   It states, in brief, that one should avoid conception during times of unusual earthly or heavenly manifestations and on days specified as ill omened.   Phallicism in China must have been practiced in T'ang or prior to it, since there is mention here of making an ivory model of the penis.   This is severely prohibited. A belief is expressed that intercourse during menstruation can lead to conception, but that the child will have a red mark as a consequence. In the Han dynasty, it was believed that the forehead of a woman who was menstruating might be marked with a red spot.   There are a few commonsensical observations directing the man not to have coitus when he needs to urinate, is overtired, or is just getting over a serious illness. The reader is warned against aphrodisiacs; this shows that aphrodisiacs were known and used in T'ang, and earlier dynasties as well.

Prohibitions

The Secrets of the Jade Bedroom states that Harmony Master Chung said: " In *The (Text of) Changes* it is stated that Heaven sends down omens as manifestations of good and evil, and that the sage patterns his behavior accordingly. In (a work dealing with) rites it is said that if one does not heed (the omen) but begets a child when thunder is about to resound, there will inevitably be a disastrous outcome. Thus it is that the sages issued their admonitions, which must be carefully heeded. If heavenly changes appear above, earthly disasters occur below. Man lives in the interval; how can he not fear and revere this? The union of the female and male elements should be especially reverent and fearful of this and careful to avoid (admonitions)."

It further states that P'eng the Methuselah said: "You must leave aside the feelings of the mundane world, and, further, avoid the extremes of cold, heat, wind, and rain, eclipses of the sun and moon, and thunder and lightning. These are Heaven's prohibitions. The human prohibitions are: to be drunken or gorged with food, joyous or angered, grieved or saddened, fearful or apprehensive. Earth's prohibitions are in the places of mountains and rivers, where the god spirits reside, the altars to the gods of soil and grain, and wells and kitchen ranges. These are Earth's prohibitions, (which include) avoidance of the three prohibitions. Those who violate these prohibitions will sicken, and their children will invariably be short-lived."

It further says, "Those who unite in intercourse when weakened from taking medicines and not yet completely cured of illness always injure themselves."

And further it says, "You shouldn't unite in intercourse when the moon is dead (i.e., the night before the new moon); it is ill omened."

It also says: "It being harmful, you shouldn't have intercourse on the (middle days of the month such as) the days of establishment, of bad omens, of taking and fixing, and of the blood prohibition."

It further states that P'eng the Methuselah said: "The reason that lechery causes you to be short-lived is not always because of the actions of demons and spirits. Women who insert powder into their vaginas or make a male stalk out of ivory and use it always injure their livers and quickly age and die."

The Illustrated Text of Frogs states that the Yellow Emperor asked the Baron of Ch'i,[68] "Why is it that men and women can get sick to-

---

68. The Baron of Ch'i was a famous medical figure of the legendary age, said to have served the Yellow Emperor. He is credited with having ascertained the medicinal properties of vegetation.

gether?" Replied the Baron: "The reason is that they have inter-course without considering the waxing and waning of the moon and the darkening and brightening of the sun, (being) unaware of the prohibi-tions concerning them. Because of this, men and women get sick together.

"You shouldn't have intercourse on the fourth and sixth days of the moon's cycle, for ulcers break out. And you shouldn't have intercourse on the ninth and fifteenth days of the moon's cycle, for the woman will be afflicted by a wind illness. Great is the prohibition. You shouldn't have intercourse on the thirtieth day, when the moon is destroyed; it is prohibited."

Hua T'o's[69] *Classic of Acupuncture and Cauterization* states: "The three days of the winter solstice, the summer solstice, and the New Year's Day, and the three days before and the two days after them are days on which acupuncture, bedroom affairs, and killings are greatly prohi-bited."[70]

The Collection of the Essentials of Nourishing Life states: "You shouldn't have intercourse during the last day of the sun and moon, when bedroom matters are prohibited; during the crescent and full moons; on the days when the six combinations of stems *ting* and *ping* are combined with characters of the twelve branches;[71] on unlucky days; on the twenty-eighth day of the lunar month; when the moon is in

---

69. Hua T'o 華佗 was a famous physician of the early third century who, having cultivated the Taoist arts, lived to be a hundred and still preserved a youthful appearance. The Wel ruler Ts'ao Ts'ao had Hua T'o killed when the latter declined to treat him once during a serious illness. Hua T'o, on the verge of execution, offered his medical work to the warden; when the warden refused it, he consigned it to the flames.

70. The connection between acupuncture and sex was in the aspect of great stimulation, believed to cause excessive movement of male-female elements on the tabooed days.

71. The Chinese system of stems and branches was one in which years and days were estimated by combining ten "celestial" stems and twelve bran-ches of horary characters in regular order, beginning with the first of each. The cycle then repeated itself after the sixtieth year or day had been reached. This way of counting in China can be traced back at least two thousand years.

eclipse; during great or severe winds, earth movements, peals of thunder and lightning, great cold or heat; on the five days before and after the start of spring, autumn, winter, and summer. There are heavy prohibitions on your birthday and on the New Year's Day. You shouldn't have intercourse during any of the following occasions: after the summer solstice, on the days *ping-tzu* and *ting-ssu*; after the winter solstice. on the days *keng-shen* and *hsin-yu*; when you have just washed your hair; when you have just gone on a distant journey and are tired; and when you are very happy or very angry. When a husband reaches his sixtieth year, the year of deterioration and forgetting, he should not emit his semen wastefully."

It further states that Ts'ui T'i of An-p'ing (also called Tzu-chen), in his *Monthly Calendar of the Four Peoples*, said that on the fifth and the mid-summer month and on the days leading up to them the female and male elements were in conflict and the blood and vapor (of the elements) did not disperse. Couples should separate for sleeping within and outside (the bedroom) on the fifth days before and after the solstices. On the eleventh and mid-autumn months and on the days leading up to them, the female and male elements were again in conflict, and there was no dispersal of blood and vapor. Couples should separate for sleeping within and outside (the bedroom) on the fifth days before and after the solstice.

It further says: "Intercourse is severely forbidden when one is drunk or gorged with food; these are great taboos. They injure man a hundredfold. If you have intercourse when drunk, it may result in ugly sores or in dizziness. Wishing to urinate but forbearing in order to have intercourse causes a man to become thoroughly soaked (with perspiration) or to have difficulty in urinating. There is an obstruction in the stalk and the abdomen hardens. You shouldn't have intercourse after you are greatly pleased or angered, for ulcers will break out."

It states further that Mr. Fortune-Teller said: "If you have intercourse with a woman before menstration has ended, you'll make her sick. If she has a child,[72] it will have a red mark affixed to its face like a hand, or it may be on its body. Furthermore, a male child will

---

72. The ancient Chinese, as far back as the Han, believed that a woman could conceive while menstruating.

get a white macular sickness (when he gets older)."

The Master of the Cave Profound said, "If a man is twice the woman's age, he harms the woman, while the woman harms the man if she is twice his age."

It further states that the Woman Plain reasoned: "One shouldn't perform the bedroom (arts) on the sixteenth day of the fifth month, for it is a day when Heaven is female and Earth is male, (reversing the usual order of things). Those who transgress against this will invariably die within three years. What means do we have of knowing this? Just take a ten-foot length of new cloth, and on this night suspend it over an eastern embankment. When you go there the next morning to look at it, it will invariably be red.[73] Earnestly taboo this."

It further says: "In looking towards intercourse, a lucky-day omen is beneficial. If you are in accord with the efficacy of the time, this will be greatly auspicious for you. Face with your head to the east in the spring; to the south in the summer; to the west in the autumn; and to the north in the winter.

"The male-element (odd-numbered) days are beneficial; the female element (even-numbered) days are harmful. Male-element time (after midnight and before noon) is beneficial; female-element time (after noon and before midnight) is harmful.

"In spring, the first and second (days); in summer, the third and fourth; in autumn, the seventh and eighth; and in winter, the ninth and tenth (days are all harmful)."

The Recipes of Priceless Gold states, "One should not enter the bedroom in the fourth and tenth months, (months in which the female and male elements use things up)."

It further states, "If you are newly fatigued, you should wash and have intercourse afterwards. Don't have intercourse unless you have washed."

And it also states: "When you have a fever and it has just gone down, or after a great illness, your vigor will not return to normal in less than

---

73. Red symbolized the woman, white the man. van Gulik (*op. cit.*, 7) notes that man was called white and woman red throughout later Chinese alchemic and erotic literature. Erotic pictures often showed man and woman in these color associations, which to him suggest that in archaic times woman was regarded as being sexually superior to man.

a hundred days. Those who nevertheless indulge in the boudoir will mostly die. A fevered boudoir is called the sickness of the interchangeability of the female and male elements. All (who transgress) are hard to cure and many die. Recently, one of the great ministers got a slight cold and it took more than ten days to cure it. He was able to ride about on horseback; saying himself that he had recovered, he indulged in the boudoir. He felt pain at once in his abdomen, his hands and feet became cramped, and he died.

" The way to cure this is to burn the place where hairs are affixed to a woman's undergarment, taking about one square teaspoonful[74] three times daily. In the case of a woman's illness, take the man's undergarment and proceed according to the same technique. Now, in Mr. Ko's prescription, it is best to get the undergarment of a female virgin.

" Still another method is to take the clothing of a woman which is worn over a place where she has had intercourse and cover the male with it for a while."

---

74. The teaspoonful described here held about 3.75 grams.

CHAPTER XXV

Introduction

This chapter explains the sex dreams of women as being dreams of coitus. The writer stresses the injuriousness to the woman who has a nocturnal emission as the result of such dreams and describes it in terms of illness, an illness which is accompanied by extreme exhaustion. The way to effect a cure, according to the Taoists, is for the woman to rub a sulphur preparation on her vagina and swallow a small amount of deer's horn powder. The use of sulphur must have been intended as a charm to induce the devil to leave, but deer's horn powder might have been used to treat neurosis, since it was believed to reduce fever and strengthen the vital fluids. In the twenty-first volume of *The Essence of Medical Prescriptions*, compiler Tamba Yasuyori included other medicinal powders taken with rice wine. He also listed prescriptions to which a tiger's claw was added, since the tiger was popularly believed to be efficacious in expelling evil spirits.

Breaking Off Intercourse with Devils

The Secrets of the Jade Bedroom states that the Woman Selective asked, " How does one get to have the illness of intercourse with devils? " Replied P'eng the Methuselah: " It comes from not having intercourse and from deepening and emphasizing one's sex desires. Then demons avail themselves of human forms and have intercourse with such persons. Since this method of intercourse is superior to that of humans, when it is practiced for a long time the human partner becomes bewitched, avoids mention of it, conceals it, and is unwilling to report it (to others). Considering this beautiful, the person therefore dies without anyone ever having discovered it. If you get this illness, the way to cure it is to make a woman have intercourse with the male, who does not emit his semen.   By not resting day or night, the one who is distressed will invariably be cured within a week.   If your body is tired and you can't control (your semen), press down deeply and don't move.   This is also good (in results).   If you don't cure this, the one who is afflicted will be dead in a few years.   Those who wish to test the truth of this should enter an area between great swamps and deep mountains in the spring and autumn.   Say and do nothing, but look afar and intensify your thoughts, concentrating solely on intercourse.   After three days and three nights, your body will be compressed by cold and heat, your heart will be troubled, your eyes will dim, and the man will see women and the woman will see men.   If you then have intercourse, its beauty will exceed that of humans.   However, this will invariably cause you to get sick, and a cure will be difficult.   There are boundless feelings of regret, and one is put to shame by the heterodox.   There will always be such persons in later generations. When virgins and women of eminence are distressed by not having intercourse with men, the way to cure this is as follows: Burn several ounces of sulphur and fumigate the woman's body below her pubic region with it.   If, at the same time, she takes a square teaspoonful of deer's horn powder, she'll be cured immediately.   You should see the demon weep and leave.   If, on the one hand, you yourself take the square teaspoonful of deer's horn powder three times a day, you will attain the right level to despatch the demon.   As for investigating ways to cure intercourse with demons, many are to be found in prescriptions listed in detail in sections (of various works) on women."

CHAPTER XXVI

Introduction

This chapter and the four that follow it deal in varying degrees with curative medicines to be taken in connection with the bedroom arts. The main emphasis in the bedroom arts is on man's achieving salvation through understanding and practicing the proper philosophical principles. But one still can make use of medicines to combat unfavorable physiological symptoms and to cope with illnesses that occur while the arts are being practiced. There are listed not only semen-strengthening recipes but also other prescriptions which merit investigation by modern researchers. Except in special instances, Chinese medical doctrine requires that all prescriptions be taken warm and on an empty stomach, usually thirty minutes to an hour before meals. The text includes a few Indian and Korean prescriptions. In two indices of medical terms, arranged by radical order of the characters or by alphabetical order of their literal meanings, there are listed the latin equivalents for the names of drugs.[75]

Making Use of Medicinal Properties

The Recipes of Priceless Gold states that the Woman Selective said, "Matters dealing with intercourse have already been heard. Now I venture to ask about taking drugs; how can one gain efficacy from them?" Replied P'eng the Methuselah: "There is nothing better than deer's horn to cause a man to be robust and unaffected by age, not to tire in the boudoir, and not to deteriorate either in energy or in

75. See the Index of Medical Terms, in which literal translations of the terms used in our text are listed, followed by Latin equivalents.

141

facial coloration. The technique is to take a reindeer's horn, cut it up to make a powder, and then combine ten ounces of it with one large raw aconite root. If you take a square teaspoonful of this three times daily, it is very good for you. You should (also) heat a tailed deer's horn till it is slightly yellow and take this by itself. It further causes a man not to get old. However, those who find it (too) slow to attain the desired effect) add an aconite root and, after taking this for twenty days, become greatly aware (of the results). One should also add fungus root from around the Lung-hsi region (in northern China), pound it into equal portions, and take a square teaspoonful of it three times daily. It causes man to live long and not to deteriorate within the bedroom."

It further says: " The following is a prescription for impotence and non-rising (of the penis); rising but not enlarging; enlarging but not lengthening; lengthening but not heating up; heating up but not hardening; hardening but not lasting: mushrooms; stalactites; parsley; the will-strengthener; marsh-plant; yams, and the soft core of the deer's antler.

" Twice daily partake of the above seven flavors in three-ounce portions each, together with rice wine. If you desire boudoir abund-ance, double the parsley; if you desire hardness, double the will-strengthener; if you desire largeness, double the soft cure of the deer's antler; if you desire an abundance of semen, double the stalactite."

The Secrets of The Jade Bedroom states: " The following is a cure when the male's penis is impotent and doesn't arise, when it arises but doesn't get strong; and when it goes forth to the event as if it had no feeling. It is the prescription to use when the male essence is slight and the source of the kidneys is weak: mushrooms and (the evergreen creeper) Five-Flavor; each in two parts. Parsley seeds; dodder seeds; and trifoliate orange seeds, each in four parts.

" The five ingredients above are to be pounded and strained and taken in a square teaspoonful three times daily along with rice wine. A Governor of Shu Commandery (in Szechwan) got a child when he was over seventy (through using this prescription).

" Further, those whose virility is not continuous should dry this (prescription given above), add three parts of the yellowish-green marshy plant (Asarum Siedollis) and three parts of parsley seeds, pound it and strain it, and blend it with sparrow eggs till it is like the dryandra seed. Take one application of this when about to have intercourse. If the penis gets strong and you can't stop it, wash it with cold water."

The Essential Instructions of the Jade Bedroom states that the following is a curative prescription to allow the male to perform healthily more than ten times a night in the boudoir, without resting: parsley; the will-strengthener; the marsh plant; and mushrooms.

The above four ingredients should be of equal amount and made into a powder. Take a square teaspoonful three times daily. Duke Ts'ao took this and had intercourse with seventy women in a single night.

The Master of the Cave Profound said: " Bald Hen Medicinal Powder is a cure for the man who, having impotence of the penis with its not rising, is incapable in the matter. Lü Ching-ta, Governor of Shu Commandery (in Szechwan), took this medicine when he was seventy and was able to beget three sons. If the prescription is taken for too long a time, it will become worrisome, with the inner part of the jade gate pained and (the woman) unable to either sit or lie down. This medicine was once left alone in a courtyard. A cock ate it, and at once got a rise and climbed on the back of a hen. He didn't get down for several days, and pecked the crown of her head bald. (That's why) it came to be called either " Bald Hen Medicinal Powder " or " Bald Hen Pills." The prescription is made up of five elements pounded and sifted into a powder, namely: three parts of salted pulpy mushrooms; three parts of Five-Flavor seeds; three parts of dodder seeds; three parts of the will-strengthener ; and four parts of parsley.

" Take a square teaspoonful of this two or three times daily with rice wine when your stomach is empty, but not unless you have a (boudoir) adversary. With it you can control forty women in sixty days. Further, mix it with white honey, make a pellet like a dryandra seed, and take five pellets twice daily. Limit your intake through awareness (of its effect)."

(He) further says: " Deer's horn medicinal powder is used as a curative when the male is repeatedly fatigued and injured; when the penis is impotent and doesn't arise ; when one goes to a woman on the spur of the moment and fails on the verge of the event; when the penis becomes impotent and dies midway along; when the semen comes forth of its own (accord); when a few drops remain after urination; and when waist and back ache and feel cold: deer's horn; juniper seed kernels; dodder seeds; parsley seeds; plantain seeds; the will-strengthener; Five-Flavor seeds; and mushrooms (each of the above in four parts).

" The above is to be pounded, sifted, and made into a powder. Take five portions in square teaspoonfuls after each meal, three times daily. If you are not aware of improvement, add another inch (of the prescription) to the teaspoonful."

The Prescriptions of Mr. Fan Wang[76] states: " The pill of the open-hearted Chinese yam and the energy of the kidneys cures the following: the constant fatigue of a man and his injuries; his body's being unable to endure severe cold; his suffering from dropsy when he goes to sleep; his stomach being filled with sounds of thunder; his losing all desire for food and drink. Even if he eats, (the food) stops completely below the heart and can't be digested. His hands are hot to a bothersome degree in spring and summer, and in winter and autumn his legs feel frozen. He is distracted and absent-minded, and his kidney energies can't function. Sexual desires don't arise but are extinguished as if he were an old man.

" If you take the following prescription, there is nothing that it will not cure. It will make one's inner organs healthy, augment the bones, fill in the emptiness, nourish the will, open the heart, tranquilize the viscera, stop tears, clear the eyes, relax the stomach, benefit the sex, remove wind, and expel cold: an ounce of salted pulpy mushrooms; an ounce of dogwood which, however, may be left out of the prescription; six parts of dried foxglove; six parts of the will-strengthener; six parts of parsley seeds; six parts of Five-Flavor seeds; six parts of a flatulency preventative; six parts of fungus root; six parts of hyssop; six parts of dodder seeds; six parts of pear tree bark; six parts of yams.

" These twelve objects are to be pounded and sifted, with honey added to make a pill like a dryandra seed. Take twenty pills twice a day and once a night, but if they bother you reduce this (amount), taking

---

76. This book, cited in the *History of Sui* (*Sui-shu* 隋書), was known in the early seventh century, but it is no longer extant. Fan Wang wrote it in 105 chapters; the complete title of the work was *Fan Tung-yang fang* 范東陽方. (For these and other details, see *Ishimpō*, 214.)

only ten pills. After you take the medicine, in five days your jade stalk will be ablaze with heat; in ten nights your whole body will be glistening and smooth; in fifteen nights your facial color will be glossy and your hands and feet always hot; in twenty nights your virile power will be on the verge of flourishing; in twenty-five nights all your veins will be full. And in thirty nights your hot vapors will be clear and thorough; your facial color will be like that of a flower; the lines in your palm will be like silk; your heart will open; and you'll retain things without forgetting. You'll do away with melancholy and stop forgetfulness; and even if you sleep alone you won't be cold. You'll put an end to (involuntary) urination and harmonize your penis. If you're under forty, one dosage will suffice; if you're over fifty, take two dosages. Though you're fully seventy years old, you can have children. There are no prohibitions, except not to eat very bitter or very sour things."

The pill (called) "salted pulpy mushroom" cures recurrent fatigues and injuries, the penis' being impotent and not arising, and having accumulations (of such debilitation) for ten years. It also cures itching and dampness, being soaked with urination, and urinating sometimes in red and other times in yellow colors. If you take this medicine, it nourishes your sex and benefits your physical energies, and it makes you healthy. (It is used) when, even in having intercourse, your penis is impotent and doesn't arise; when it arises but doesn't get hard; when it gets hard but doesn't get angry; when it gets angry but is irresolute; and when it enters but then dies of its own accord. This medicine augments the semen, benefits your physical vigor, and makes your facial color fine and you yourself corpulent and white: four portions each of salted pulpy mushrooms; dodder seeds; parsley seeds; Five-Flavor seeds; the will-strengthener; marsh plant; and pear tree bark.

The seven ingredients above are to be pounded and sifted, mixed with honey, and made into a pill shaped like a dryandra seed. Take five pills at dawn and kneel down twice during the day and face the east.[77] If you are unaware of a difference from the pills, you can take

---

77. There was a Taoist custom of absorbing energy from the east; hence this reference.

up to seven of them. If you take them, in thirty days you'll become aware (of difference), and in fifty days your sex will greatly arise. If your sex is weak, add more parsley seeds; if it doesn't get angry, add more will-strengthener; if the semen is scant in quantity, add more Five-Flavor seeds. If you want the penis to become vastly enlarged, add more mushrooms; to (cure) soreness of the waist, add more pear tree bark; and if you want to make the penis longer, add more of the marsh plant. The way to add to these is to double the amounts.

Even if an old gentleman of eighty takes this, he'll become like a thirty-year-old. Test it by using it several times, but don't take it when you're womanless. The prohibitions (concerning indulging in sex with women) are as usual.

The pill called the will-strengthener, is a cure for the man's seven injuries and for the sex being impotent and not arising: four ounces of the marsh plant; two ounces of yams; two ounces of the will-strengthener; two ounces of parsley seeds; and two ounces of salted pulpy mushrooms.

These five ingredients are to be put through a fine sieve, mixed with sparrow eggs, and made into pills shaped like beans. Take five pills at dawn and twice a day; the penis will get to be an inch longer in a hundred days and three inches longer in two hundred days.

Recipes (Based on) Recorded Experiences states: " There is a benefit to many medicines. This maiden, your concubine, bows again and again and presents writings to His Celestial Majesty. She bows her head, deserving death for her crimes. She has heard it said that the highest good is not prohibited. Her husband, Hua Fou, at eighty, having deteriorated in bedroom matters, learned about the following prescription:

" Wash and slice thinly fresh foxglove and saturate it with a pint of clear rice wine. When it has been saturated, pound it a thousand times into a powder. Allow it (to be mixed) with a foot[78] (two parts) of cinnamon bark, fire it with five parts of licorice root, and use two parts of glutinous millet and five parts of dried lacquer.

These five ingredients are to be beaten into a powder, put through a fine sieve, and cured together and made to blend. Take a square tea-

---

78. This referred to the weight, as well as the length, of the tree bark.

spoonful with rice wine after meals three times daily. Hua Fou blended this medicine and had not yet (finished) taking (the complete course as prescribed) when his illness vanished.

" He had a slave, to whom he gave the name of Benefits Many. At seventy-five he was sickly, with bent waist and whitened hair, and he walked about sideways and hunchbacked. Your concubine felt pity over this and gave the medicine to Benefits Many. He took it and in twenty days his waist strengthened, his white hair turned black, his facial color became smooth and glossy, and he looked like a thirty-year-old. Your concubine had two maids called Barbarian At Rest and Attentively Good, whom Benefits Many took as wives, and they bore him four boys and girls. He once went out to drink rice wine, returned introxicated, and hurried to take Attentively Good, who was lying at my side. Benefits Many caught up with her and they had intercourse. I woke up and listened covertly; he abounded in physical energy and virile movement and was slightly different from other males. I am fifty, but I opened the boudoir (to him) and was remiss, (though I was widowed) and unacquainted with other men. I was unable to eradicate my womanly feelings and I gave birth twice. Benefits Many had intercourse in a totally uninhibited way with me and the two maids, but we became ashamed and killed him. When we broke open his shinbone and looked within, it was filled with yellow marrow;[79] we realized this was evidence of the prescription. If Your Majesty uses this ointment in controlling (women) your bones will be filled with marrow and for you it will be a good and proper prescription. Your concubine, deserving death, bows her head again and again; may (her memorial) be heard."

Recipes of Extreme Essentials states that there is a prescription for curing the male, increasing his boudoir vigor a hundredfold, and enabling him to always have ample semen, with his life-force benefitted and a hot and large sex arousal secured: two parts of parsley seeds; two parts of dodder seeds; two parts of the holly; two parts of salted pulpy mushrooms; one part of the will-strengthener (removing the heart of it); one part of Five-Flavor seeds; and one part of a flatulency preventative.

---

79. Chinese physicians believe that extremely healthy persons have yellow marrow in their bones. In China, old people may be referred to as being withered in bones; in other words, their bones lack the yellow marrow.

Make the above into a medicinal powder, taking about a half-copper amount of it with rice wine; and in twenty days your semen energy will be benefitted.

In *The Recipes of Mr. Ko*, there is a prescription for male impotence, frigidity of the woman's vagina, and failure to return to the human way: one ounce each of salted pulpy mushrooms; parsley seeds; the will-strengthener; marsh plant; and dodder seeds.

Pound these to a powder, and take a square teaspoonful with rice wine three times daily.

It further says: " This is the prescription for one who, (although) usually strong, weakens when about to have intercourse. Make parsley seeds and dodder seeds into a powder and take a square teaspoonful of it with rice wine three times daily."

The Recipes of Jivāka[80] records a prescription for curing impotence; one part each of aspen, calamus, and dodder seeds. Mix these, put them through a fine strainer, and take a square teaspoonful three times daily. You'll get to be as hard and as strong as an iron pestle.

Another prescription: Early at dawn, on an empty stomach, put good quality thyme into warm rice wine and drink it.

Another prescription: Make a powder from parsley seeds alone and drink it with rice wine.

The annotation by Su Ching (completed in 659) to the *Pen-ts'ao*[81] (Materia Medica) states, " For impotence, dry yams daily. Pound and strain, make into a powder, and eat."

The Silla Dharma Master Flowing View states in his *Secret Essential Recipes* that he received the following prescription from Favored and Loyal, the great T'ang state's Dharma Master from Ching-ch'eng District in Ts'ang Prefecture (i.e., modern Hopei's Ts'ang District).

---

80. Jivāka was the son of King Bimbisāra who became renowned for his medical skills. At birth he was said to have seized the acupuncture needle and bag. Jivāka was also the name of one of eight principal drugs. (Soothill, *A Dictionary of Chinese Buddhist Terms*, 326, 336.)

81. Su Ching 蘇敬 was ordered to annotate a *Pen-ts'ao* 本草 (Materia Media) of the T'ang by Emperor Kao-tsung, and he completed his work in 659. (*Ishimpō*, 223.) There are many references to his annotations in the extant Ming compilation *Pen-ts'ao kang-mu* 本草綱目, which contains extracts from the medical treatises of about 800 writers.

Said Favored and Loyal: " *The Record of Experiences of the Dharma Treasure* states: ' The Tathagata Buddha preserved this prescription in order to profit the masses, but the masses were ignorant and didn't desire it. That is why it was not widely known. On a day when (the Buddhist Messiah) Maga-puspa and (the Brahmin Buddhist convert) Asvaghosa found it difficult to explain the Buddha's teachings, they achieved awareness only of this medicine. They transmitted (this knowledge) forthwith to a Sramana ascetic, but the ascetic was shamed by it, and he transmitted it no further; therefore, it is not possessed by the world.

' When the Beneficial King was ruling the kingdom of Western India, a (spirit) man from Purva Terrace (in the east) called Asura, about a foot, two inches high, flew in on the wind. He offered up the essential prescriptions containing the secrets of the twelve great vows and the three excellences When the King reverently looked them over, they consisted of the instructions of the Buddha Tathagata, the Medicine Master. The King then liked the curative arts and here he obtained evidences (of such cures) several times. He further received an immense fortune beyond (his realm) and enfeoffments in sixteen great states.

' He controlled innumerable consorts. Each and every one of them was fragrantly adorned and they pleased him one and all, with none wayward in heart. One could not transmit through a thousand gold pieces the loftiness of his virtue and the splendor of his benevolence.' "

Secret Recipes of the Silla Dharma Master states: " During the middle ten days of the eighth (lunar) month, take an exposed beehive, place a level object on (top of) it, and let it press down on the beehive for one night. Then take the beehive and put it into a silk bag. Hang this on a bamboo pole and dry it in the shade for a hundred days; it will then become a wondrous medicine for time unlimited.

" Now when you're looking forward to intercourse cut it up and, taking a piece about the size of six coppers, put it into a clear full earthen jar and boil it. It will pass through a stage of black ashes and become white ashes. Then put half of it in warm rice wine and swallow it. Put the other half in your hand, mix it with your saliva, and dab it on the bones of the buttocks from beginning to end. When you have finished dabbing it on, it will soon dry. When it dries, you can have intercourse as your heart desires. If you continue taking it for forty days, there will gradually be signs (of its efficacy). At the end of a hundred days, your body will be completely regulated. Until the end of your life, you'll have benefits and no injuries. There will be blessings and virtues ten thousandfold and physical energies sevenfold; you'll get whatever you seek and have an illness-free longevity. In the heat of summer (the medicine) beckons coolness, and in the prime of winter it pursues warmth. It guards against evil vapors, and calamities are not encountered. It is a so-called accumulator of increased benefits. If you apply it to the buttocks one hundred and eighty times vertically and horizontally, (your penis) will get as strong as an iron pestle and grow three inches larger. The feces will naturally become fragrant; shrink them and place them in a utensil. Men and women (after taking the medicine) become quiescent in spirit and discerning in heart, keen of hearing and bright eyed, with fragrant mouth and nose vapors.

Strength-seekers should always place (the medicine) in warm rice wine and then drink it; length-seekers should dab it on their extremities; while largeness-seekers should dab it all around. You are forbidden to drink it when experiencing extreme states of sadness, pleasure, fright, remorse, and inactivity; when you are perspiring from running quickly; during a flood; or when you are on a preciptious height. Also prohibited are the five spices, foods that are greasy and cold, raw vegetables, and getting drunk. Now here there is already a prescription for strengthening the penis; it can also be used beforehand to guard against deterioration.''

The Recipes of Mr. Ko speaks of a prescription for causing one's sex to become impotent and weak. Take mercury, the soft core of the deer's antler, and croton oil beans, and mix and pound together into a powder. Blend into this genuine tailed deer's fat; affix it to the penis and scrotum, and wrap it all around with silk. If the fat is (too) strong, boil it together with hemp oil. This is no different from (the formula used by) the eunuchs.[82] Now one simply makes the mercury into a powder and dabs it on (penis and scrotum). There is another prescrip-

---

82. This may be the earliest recorded reference in China to a formula used in castration. In ancient Rome, mercury was also mentioned as something which weakened the penis. (See Dioscorides' *Materia Media*.)

tion in which one cauterizes a hole at the junction point of the three male elements and causes deterioration and weakening of the male's virile powers. This hole is located three inches[83] above the inside of the ankle.

Mr. Su Ching says, in his annotation to the *P'en-ts'ao* (Materia Medica), "Tailed deer's fat should not be placed near the male's sex." T'ao Hung-ching (456–536) says, in his annotation to the *Pen-ts'ao* (Materia Medica): "Once water-caltrop nuts are covered with frost, eating them will weaken the penis."

---

83. The original text recorded *eight* in error for *three.* (See Dr. Ishihara's annotation in *Ishimpō,* 227.)

CHAPTER XXVII

Introduction

This chapter introduces three methods for alleviating smallness of the penis, two of which are external. As already noted, Chinese medicines are usually taken before each meal and on an empty stomach, but here the user is directed to take the mixture after meals. Judging from the ingredients, it is very doubtful that an effect was achieved, as claimed.

Smallness of the Jade Stalk

Essential Instructions for the Jade Bedroom records a prescription for curing the male, causing his penis to get larger: five parts of juniper seed kernels; four parts of white sorrel; seven parts of white glutinous millet; three parts of cinnamon bark; and one part of aconite seeds.

Make the above five ingredients into a powder and take a square teaspoonful twice daily after meals. If you take it twenty times in ten days, your penis will get larger.

Secrets of the Jade Bedroom records a prescription for the man who wishes to enlarge his penis: prickly ash; yellowish-green marshy plant; the herb (which looks like a mallow); and salted pulpy mushrooms.

Measure equal amounts of these three flavors, put them through a fine strainer, and insert them in a dog's gallbladder. Hang this up for thirty days in a room in the place in which you're living. If you then rub it on the penis, it will get an inch larger.

The Master of the Cave Profound speaks of a prescription for elongating the penis, consisting of three parts of salted pulpy mushrooms and two parts of medicinal sea onions. These are to be pounded, strained, made into a powder, and blended in the first (lunar) month with the liver juices of a white dog.   (According to him), if you dab it on the penis three times and wash it off at dawn with fresh well water, your penis will get three inches longer.   It is extremely efficacious.

CHAPTER XXVIII

Introduction

This chapter should be consulted together with part of the twenty-first section of *The Essence of Medical Prescriptions*, which also discusses ways to cure largeness of the vagina. There are five prescriptions given here, as compared with six in the twenty-first section. Two of the prescriptions are identical, but the texts differ.[84]

Largeness of the Jade Gate

Instructions for the Jade Bedroom speaks of a prescription for making the woman's jade gate smaller; it consists of four parts of sulphur and two parts of the will-strengthener. This is to be made into a medicinal powder. Fill a silk purse with it; if you affix this to the inside of the jade gate tightening results will be achieved. Another prescription is to make a medicinal powder of two parts each of sulphur and rush blossoms. Then mix three fingersful into a pint of hot water and wash the jade gate with it. In twenty days she'll be like an unmarried maiden.

The Master of the Cave Profound speaks of a prescription for curing the expansiveness and coldness of a woman's vagina, making it urgent, small, and pleasurably suited for intercourse. It consists of two parts each of crude sulphur; a (special) evergreen tree fragrance; dogwood; and dodder seeds. The four ingredients are to be pounded, strained, and made into a powder. Approaching intercourse, insert a little of it

---

84. The twenty-first section refers to the danger of using even one spoonful too much of the prescription, while the twenty-eighth section refers not to spoonsful but to fingersful, thereby avoiding the danger of prescribing too large a quantity.

inside the jade gate—it should not be applied excessively, for there is a danger that the hole will get completely blocked.

Here is another prescription. Take three fingersful of crude sulphur and place it in a pint of hot water. If you wash the vagina with this, you'll quickly become like a twelve-or thirteen-year-old girl.

Recipes (Based on) Recorded Experience records a prescription for rapidly making a woman's vagina small and hot, consisting of two parts of evergreen tree fragrance and four parts of dogwood. Make these two ingredients into a medicinal powder and blend it with saliva until it looks like a small bean. Insert it inside the jade gate, and there will be wondrous efficacy.

CHAPTER XXIX

Introduction

This chapter and the concluding one form a pair, both dealing with the pain suffered by women because of coitus; but here the young and inexperienced female is considered. The six prescriptions given are the same as those recorded in the twenty-first section, under the sub-heading, *Ways To Cure the Pain of a Woman With a Small Entrance Who Marries*. A few of the words differ but there are only minor discrepancies in the two texts concerning the amounts of the medicines to be prescribed. This chapter also gives treatments for undue bleeding, as well as pain, when the woman comes into "transgression with the principle of male virility."

A Maiden's Pain

Recipes (Based on) Recorded Experiences records a curative prescription for the young girl when she first has intercourse, including her coming into transgression with the principle of male virility, her being injured by other things, and her bleeding in an unstopping flow. Burn up disheveled hair together with pieces of indigo cloth and make a powder. If you apply this powder there will be an immediate improvement. Another prescription calls for dabbing on hemp oil, while for still another prescription one takes carbon from the bottom of a pot, breaks up a bottle-gourd, and rubs and dabs these on. *Recipes of Priceless Gold* records a prescription for curing the marital pain of the little gate.[85] Burn two black cuttlefish bones into a fine powder and take a square teaspoonful of it with rice wine three times daily. Another prescription

---

85. A metaphor for the labia minora.

consists of five ounces of hyssop, to be boiled in three pints of rice wine and then boiled a second time. Remove the dregs and divide the remainder into three portions. *Secrets of the Jade Bedroom* tells of a curative prescription for the woman who, on first having intercourse, experiences pain for days unending. It consists of two parts of licorice root; two parts of herbaceous peony; three parts of raw ginger; and ten parts of cinnamon. Boil the ingredients in three pints of water, reboil them three times, and drink them down at once.

CHAPTER XXX

Introduction

The last chapter describes how an older woman can cure the pains that arise when she is subject to boudoir excesses. The four prescriptions given here are similar to those in the twenty-first section of *The Essence of Medical Prescriptions*, but they are given in a slightly different order. Additional ways to alleviate pain are recorded in *Recipes of Priceless Gold*. Medical cures such as these are considered supplementary bedroom measures. In the prescriptions, powdered medicines figure most frequently, pills are next most commonly used, but boiled preparations are rarely prescribed.

Pains of the Older Woman

Secrets of the Jade Bedroom tells of a prescription for the woman who is injured by her husband's excessive intercourse and distressed by swelling of the vagina and by aches and pains. It consists of white bark from a mulberry root, cut down to half an ounce; an ounce of dried ginger; an ounce of cinnamon bark, and twenty jujubes. These are boiled in a gallon of rice wine and then reboiled three times; one pint is to be swallowed. One is cautioned not to perspire or be exposed to the wind. Boiled water can be used (in place of the wine).

Recipes (Based on) Recorded Experience tells of a curative prescription for the woman who is harmed by a man and whose four limbs become sunken weights—she suffers from breathlessness and headaches. It consists of eight ounces of raw foxglove; five ounces of herbaceous peony; one pint of fermented black beans; one pint of the cut white roots of onions; four ounces of fresh ginger; and two ounces of dried licorice root. Cut up each one and cook them all in seven pints; take the three pints (remaining after further boiling) and divide into three portions. If there is no change (in your condition) prepare it once again.

Recipes of Priceless Gold tells of a prescription for curing unbearable sudden pain felt during intercourse. It consists of six parts of bitter rhizomes (of Coptis teeta); four parts of hyssop; and four parts of licorice root. The three flavors are to be boiled in four pints of water; take the two pints (remaining after further boiling) and wash with this (mixture) four times daily.

The Immortal's Recipes tells of a prescription for when the woman suddenly bleeds during intercourse. It is made up of two parts of cinnamon bark and three parts of crouching dragon liver (a metaphor for the purplish clay found at the bottom of old kitchen pots). Take a square teaspoonful of the two flavors in rice wine three times daily.

Index of Sex Terms*

Literal Meaning	Medical Meaning	Chinese Characters
angry	erectile penis	怒
to arise	erectile penis	起
cave	vagina	洞
child door	uterus	子戸
child gate	vagina	子門
child palace	uterus	子宮
cinnabar hole	vagina	丹穴
dark garden	prepuce of the clitoris	玄圃
death	non-erectile	死
gate	vagina	門
gate and door	vagina	門戸
god field	prepuce of the clitoris	神田
golden ditch	upper part of the vulva	金溝
grain seed	glans clitoris	穀實
heavenly court	vestibular fossa	天庭
the hidden place	vagina	隱處
hill of sedge	mons pubis	莎崗
infant girl	vestibular glands	嬰女
jade door	vagina	玉戸
jade gate	vagina	玉門
jade object	penis	玉物
jade terrace	clitoris	璿台
jade vein	the place below the vulva where the labia meet	玉理
lute strings	frenulum of the clitoris	琴絃
male vanguard	penis	陽鋒
mixed rock	vestibular glands	昆石
the mouse in the empty boat	clitoris	俞鼠

---

* Listed by alphabetical order of literal meanings.

negative—positive	female—male elements	陰陽
odoriferous mouse	vaginal secretion	臭鼠
red chamber	uterus	朱室
red pearl	labium minor	赤珠
returning the semen	non-ejaculation	還精
royal college	the left and right sides of the vulva	辟雍
seed	clitoris	實
solitary valley	vestibular fossa	幽谷
strong enemy	woman as a man's sexual adversary	強敵
sun terrace	vestibular glands	陽台
vast stream	external urethral orifice	鴻泉
wheat buds	labium minor	麥齒

Index of Sex Terms (2) *

Chinese Characters	Literal Meaning	Medical Meaning
丹穴	cinnabar hole	vagina
俞鼠	the mouse in the empty boat	clitoris
幽谷	solitary valley	vestibular fossa
天庭	heavenly court	vestibular fossa
嬰女	infant girl	vestibular glands
子宮	child palace	uterus
子戶	child door	uterus
子門	child gate	vagina
實	seed	clitoris
強敵	strong enemy	woman as a man's sexual adversary
怒	angry	erectile penis

* Listed by dictionary order of radicals.

昆石	mixed rock	vestibular glands
朱室	red chamber	uterus
死	death	non-erectile penis
穀實	grain seed	glans clitoris
洞	cave	vagina
鴻泉	vast stream	external urethral orifice
玄圃	dark garden	prepuce of the clitoris
玉戶	jade door	vagina
玉物	jade object	penis
玉理	jade vein	the place below the vulva where the labia meet
玉莖	jade stalk	penis
玉門	jade gate	vagina
琴絃	lute strings	frenulum of the clitoris
璿台	jade terrace	clitoris
神田	god field	prepuce of the clitoris
臭鼠	odoriferous mouse	vaginal secretion
莎崗	hill of sedge	mons pubis
赤珠	red pearl	labium minor
起	to arise	erectile penis
辟雍	royal college	the left and right sides of the vulva
還精	returning the semen	non-ejaculation
金溝	golden ditch	upper part of the vulva
門	gate	vagina
門戶	gate and door	vagina
陽台	sun terrace	vestibular glands
陽鋒	male vanguard	penis
隱處	the hidden place	vagina
陰陽	negative—positive	female—male elements
麥齒	wheat buds	labium minor

Index of Medical Terms*

*   Listed by alphabetical order of literal meanings.

marsh plant	Codonopsis pilosula	續斷
(medicinal) sea onions	Sargassum pallidum	海藻
mercury	Hydrargyrum	水銀
mulberry tree root	Morus bombycis	桑根
mushrooms	Cistanche salsa	蓯蓉
parsley	Cnidium monnieri	蛇床
parsley seeds	,,　　　　,,	蛇床子
pear tree bark	Eucommia ulmoides	杜仲
herbaceous peony	Paeonia albiflora	芍藥
plantain seeds	Plantago major	車前子
prickly ash	Xanthoxylum piperitum	蜀椒
raw aconite root	Aconitum chinense	生附子
raw foxglove	Rehmannia glutinosa	生地黄
rush blossoms	Typha latifolia	蒲華
salted pulpy mushrooms	Cistanche salsa	肉蓯蓉
soft core of a deer's antler	Cornu Cervi parvum	鹿茸
sulphur	Sulphur	硫黄
stalactite	Stalactitum	鐘乳 or 鐘乳(石)
tailed deer's fat	Adeps Cervi	麋脂
tailed deer's horn	Cornu Cervi	麋角
thyme	Perilla ocymoides	蘇
trifoliate orange seeds	Citrus ichangensis	枳實
water caltrop nuts	Trapa bispinosa	芰實
white glutinous millet	Atractylis lancea	白朮
white onion hearts	Allium fistulosum	葱白
white sorrel	Ampelopsis japonica	白斂
the will-strengthener	Polygala sibirica	遠志
yam	Dioscorea japonica	薯蕷
yellowish-green marshy plant	Asiasarum sieboldi	細辛

Index of Medical Terms (2)

Chinese Characters	Literal Meaning	Latin Equivalent
乾地黃	dried foxglove	Rehmannia glutinosa
乾漆	dried lacquer	Rhus verniciflua
乾薑	dried ginger	Zingiber officinale
五味	Five-Flavor (evergreen creeper)	Schizandra chinensis
五味子	Five-Flavor seeds	″ ″
伏龍肝	crouching dragon liver	Terra flava usta
兎絲子	dodder seeds	Cuscuta japonica
小麻油	hemp oil	Oleum sesami
山茱萸	dogwood	Cornus officinalis
巴戟天皮	holly	Herpestris monniera
巴豆	croton oil beans	Croton tiglium
朮	glutinous millet	Atractylis lancea
杜仲	pear tree bark	Eucommia ulmoides
枳實	trifoliate orange seeds	Citrus ichangensis
枸杞	aspen	Lisium chinese
柏子仁	juniper seed kernels	Biota orientalis
桑根	mulberry tree root	morus bombycis
桂心	cinnamon bark preparation	Cinnamomum cassia
梧子	dryandra seeds	Sterculia platanifolia
棗	jujubes	Zizyphus vulgaris
水銀	mercury	Hydrargyrum
海藻	(medicinal) sea onions	Sargassum pallidum
烏賊魚骨	black cuttle fish bones	Sepin esculenta
牛膝	hyssop	Achyranthes aspera
甘草	licorice root	Glycyrrhiza glabra
生地黃	raw foxglove	Rehmannia glutinosa
生薑	ginger root	Zingiber officinale
生附子	raw aconite root	Aconitum chinense

---

* Listed by dictionary order of radicals.

166

白朮	white glutinous millet	Atractylis lancea
白斂	white sorrel	Ampelopsis japonica
硫黃	sulphur	Sulphur
細辛	yellow-green marshy plant	Asiasarum sieboldi
續斷	marsh plant	Codonopsis pilosula
蜀椒	prickly ash	Xanthoxylum piperitum
肉蓯蓉	salted pulpy mushrooms	Cistanche salsa
芍藥	herbaceous peony	Paeonia albiflora
芰實	water-caltrop nuts	Trapa bispinosa
茯苓	fungus root	Pachyma cocos
菖蒲	calamus	Acorus gramineus
葱白	white onion hearts	Allium fistulosum
蒲華	rush blossoms	Typha latifolia
蓯蓉	mushrooms	Cistanche salsa
薯蕷	yam	Dioscorea japonica
蘇	thyme	Perilla ocymoides
蛇床	parsley	Cnidium monnieri
蛇床子	parsley seeds	” ”
車前子	plantain seeds	Plantago major
遠志	the will-strengthener	Polygala sibirica
鐘乳 or 鐘乳(石)	stalactite	Stalactitum
防風	flatulency preventative	Siler diva licatum
附子	aconite root	Aconitum chinense
青木香	evergreen tree fragrance	Aucklandia costus
香豉	fermented black beans	Semen Sojae
鹿茸	soft core of a deer's antler	Cornu Cervi parvum
鹿角	deer's horn	Cornu Cervi
麋脂	tailed deer's fat	Adeps Cervi
麋角	tailed deer's horn	Cornu Cervi
黃連	bitter rhizomes	Coptis teeta

Appendices

One: Chinese Medicine as Practised in Japan*

Chinese medicine formed one of the main currents of Japanese medical practice for more than a thousand years, from about a century before the T'ang dynasty till the end of the Tokugawa era.   It came to Japan via Korea and, while absorbing indigenous elements, enjoyed a rise to popularity commensurate with the way in which Buddhism came to flourish on Japanese soil.   Due to frequent Sino-Japanese scholarly exchanges, Sui-T'ang (587–906) medicinal arts became firmly rooted in Japan; in 701, the Japanese authorities promulgated an exact copy of China's medical system.   In general, there was an uncritical acceptance of everything T'ang, including medicine.

In the eighth century, Japan was also introduced to medical practices originating in India and the Middle East.   A break-off in Sino-Japanese cultural relations in the aftermath of the Huang Ch'ao rebellion of 875 led to a temporary resurgence in favor of indigenous medical practices. Less than twenty years later, however, in 894, a publication event occurred that assured Chinese medicine of a dominant place in Japan for the next millenium.   It was then that Tamba Yasuyori, a court physician of Chinese lineage, issued *The Essence of Medical Prescriptions* (*Ishimpō*), a Han-Sui-T'ang compendium which faithfully recorded hundreds of extracts from Chinese medical texts.   Enjoying imperial patronage, this compendium was destined to earn an eminent position as the oldest work of its kind extant in Japan.

With the organization of the Kamakura Shogunate in 1184, social reforms were instituted, and in the medical field there was a move away

---

* A condensation of Dr. Ishihara's writings; cf. " *Kampō: Japan's Traditional Medicine*," (Japan Quarterly, Vol. IX, No. 4, 1962), *Nihon no Igaku* 日本の医学 (Shibundō 至文堂, Tokyo, 1966).

from subservience to Sui-T'ang models towards absorption of the more practical medicine of the Sung (960–1279). Tamba Yasuyori's descendants, however, simply wrote studies based on *Ishimpō* and failed to open new paths of development. During the Kamakura era, many health centers were set up in temples, and medicine became a monopoly of the priestly class. In the next few centuries medicine began to reflect social trends with increasing clarity and an empiric medicine developed among the masses. The diffusion of medical information and the trend towards empiricism brought about the decline of Sui-T'ang classical theorists, who stressed theory but slighted practice. Physicians sent to Ming China (1368–1643) introduced a new system of thought, and medicine in Japan once again came to form a medley of elements, including Korean as well as Chinese. These were set in order by Manase Dōsan (1507–94), a celebrated physician of Confucian leanings who based his methods on clinical experience, completely rejecting Buddhist religious elements. He advocated careful prescribing for each patient's ills. Setting up a medical school at his own expense, he founded a group known as the *Goseiha* 後世派, which constituted an important influence till the end of the Tokugawa age.

It was in Tokugawa that Confucianism came to form the ideological spirit behind learning and, in medicine, an idea gained ground that Confucianism and medical science were identical in spirit. The close identification of medicine with this anti-empiric philosophical element led to a counter-reaction. Progressive physicians of the day criticized the theoretical involvement of the *Goseiha* and called for a reversion in orientation to ancient Chinese medical practices. They particularly advocated the system of practical therapy instituted in Han China, in which drug therapy formed the nucleus, and they came to be called " The Sect of Ancient Prescriptions " (*Kohōha* 古方派). Their school developed a system of clinical medicine based strictly on the physician's experiences, with decisions reached according to the methodology set forth in ancient Chinese medical works.

" The Sect of Ancient Prescriptions " divided into two groups, each called by the name of a medical leader. The Yoshimasu Tōdō (1702–73) school developed a homeopathic approach, using drugs similar in nature to that of the disease. This was one approach; the Yamawaki Tōyō (1705–62) school moved in the directions of observation and dissection and in 1754 carried out the first dissection in Japan of a human body for medical purposes. The Japanese checked the observations in a Dutch book on anatomy with their own, and were astonished by the similarity of the findings. Their pioneering efforts led the way for the introduction of Western medicine into Japan in 1771 by Sugita Gempaku (1733–1817).

The Yoshimasu school ignored basic medical theory and concentrated on clinical aspects. It became increasingly dogmatic, insisted that poison be used to attack the poison of a disease, and used drugs with drastic effects. Its methodological shortcomings prevented this school from achieving further development.

In the latter part of Tokugawa, the " Sect of Ancient Prescriptions " controlled the mainstream of Chinese medicine, stressing two dissimilar tendencies. It advocated empiricism in research but at the same time tried to adapt classical theories to medical practice. Scholarly involvement estranged the school from making further empirical discoveries. With the Meiji Restoration, enthusiasm for Western medicine led to a severe setback for traditional practices.

In the Meiji era, Chinese medical practitioners in Japan lost ground because their methods of treatment lacked a scientific element of universal applicability. Despite its therapeutic merits, Chinese medicine could not be applied on a broad impersonal scale, as it depended on the relationship between patient and doctor and the doctor's perception and intuition concerning the patient's ills, seen against a context of the total being. The spirit in Japan was to catch up with the West by adopting aspects of its social structure, a process in which the spirit of Chinese medicine proved incompatible.

After 1895, it became legally impossible for a physician to get authorization to practice Chinese medicine alone. Two other important allied theories, acupuncture and moxibustion, were similarly ostracized by being accorded special status as practices in which the blind would be given priority.

The value of Chinese medicine, however, is today gradually being realized. At the turn of the century, pharmacological analyses of its medical components achieved results, and in the 1920's new awareness was achieved of the electro-physiological efficacy of acupuncture and moxibustion. And in 1927 a study was made which viewed ancient prescriptions in a modern terminological context. Interested Japanese doctors worked towards the revival of Chinese medicine, but academic circles proved unsympathetic, and it was not until 1940 that a university course was offered. Even in 1968, despite the resurgence of interest, courses on Chinese medicine are not offered in Japan's medical colleges and attendance at private schools offers the only effective recourse for securing information and guidance. There are about 120,000 doctors in Japan, but of this number only about eighty are qualified Chinese medical practitioners. This problem is compounded by the fact that the post-war educated Japanese is unable to read with facility the ancient Chinese medical texts which provide theoretical bases for modern clinical practices.

There is currently a resurgence of interest in Chinese medicine because of its clinical significance. It does not designate diseases as in the West, but instead sets down a list of conditions that have to be present before a specific prescription (combining two or more drugs) can be used. If, for example, six conditions are listed, the prescription may be given to a patient who suffers from at least half of the conditions. This means that one prescription may be used to treat what in the West might be a wide range of illnesses. Further, the Chinese medical practitioner is expected to make a correct evaluation of the symptoms at each stage in the disease—he grasps the " image " of the disease and treats it according to the totality of symptoms. In order to prescribe, he has to find a treatment to match the conditions of the patient, and an essential intangible in the process is the doctor's experience in handling patients over a long period. This concept of diagnosis is probably the most important contribution that Chinese medicine can make to its Western counterpart. Modern medicine would gain by following the insistence of the Chinese diagnostician that the appropriate conditions be made clear for the taking of each medicine.

As regards acupuncture and moxibustion, the basic idea behind these therapies is to adjust an imbalance—between plus and minus elements believed to constitute the sources of all forms of life energy. This method of treatment, which originated in ancient China in the Yellow River region, posits twelve streams of vital energy. Recent developments in electrophysiology tend to support this hypothesis by showing that, by and large, changes in the skin's electrical resistance correspond to these twelve energy streams.   In acupuncture, the flesh at particular points is pierced with fine needles of a type used in sewing silk, with the effectiveness depending on the patient's reaction to the stimulus.   In moxibustion, a special substance called *mogusa* (young dried mugwort leaves) is burned on the skin surface to attain a heat stimulation and chemical effect.   In technique, the physician first takes the patient's pulse to see whether the specific vital energy source is adequate, after which he applies the stimulus at particular points in order to adjust the balance of vital forces.   These forms of treatment are especially efficacious in cases involving pain and paralysis.

Why does Chinese medicine still survive today, alongside Western medicine?   Because it is effective and practical.   A number of Chinese drugs were analyzed in the past, but the complex structure of herbal components made data on the comprehensive effect of prescriptions extremely difficult to obtain.   However, advances in biochemical research have now made it possible to clarify the special characteristics of Chinese herbs and interest has been heightened in their capacities as crude extracts of complex drugs.   Chinese drugs have the same stable structure as our daily foods, which makes them very easy to digest, and they lack the irritability of chemical structures.   The East manifested its wisdom through the realization that the total effect of natural products in combination is more than the sum of their individual effects. Elucidation of these effects is a major task for pharmacology.

Acupuncture and moxibustion are being put into practice in France and Germany without undue difficulty, but diffusion of Chinese prescriptions is a much more complex problem.   More than half of the drugs have to be imported from China, through Hong Kong.   But because of political unrest on the mainland in Yunnan and Szechwan, major centers of Chinese herbal ingredients, the herbs are getting harder to obtain. Therefore, the more popular Chinese medicine becomes, the greater will be the imbalance between supply and demand.   (Japan now imports about $45 million dollars worth yearly of Chinese herbal materials.) The next difficulty is that it is hard to standardize prescriptions, since there are no legal specifications for the drugs.   Also, modern man is in too much of a hurry to observe the general rule governing Chinese drugs, namely that they be infused in a leisurely way and with warm water.   Most prescriptions increase the frequency of bowel movements, which may cause considerable inconvenience. In Japan, successful ways have been found to produce handy ready-made prescriptions, mass-producing them in either powdered or granular forms. Future improvements in manufacture should result in a still more perfect product.

Chinese medicine remains therapeutic and individual, with the patient-physician relationship paramount. Hence it demands much of the physician in terms of insights and understanding and it lacks an element of universal scientific applicability. It does not easily fit in with an academic curriculum, nor does it lend itself to popularization through mass media techniques. These factors prevent it from linking up with modern medicine and inhibit its potential for further development. Despite these negative factors, Chinese herbs, acupuncture, and moxibustion are being seriously studied in Japan and elsewhere. They are being put to practical use, not because of sentiment or nostalgia for the esoteric East, but because they are of practical use.

Two: Levy-Ishihara Dialogue on Chinese Medicine*

Ishihara: The following is a discussion of the chapter on medicine recorded in the 28th section of *The Essence of Medical Prescriptions* (*Ishimpō*).

Levy: Tonight I should like to ask you a few questions about the differences between Chinese and Western medicine. For example, when foreigners speak about Chinese medicine, they think of the ways that snakes and all sorts of weird ingredients are used, but what is the real situation?

Ishihara: Even the Japanese react that way, equating it with the mysterious and the shamanistic. They too have an image of unusual ingredients that are hard to obtain but extremely efficacious. However, when you think of its origin in China it becomes understandable as to why such concepts exist. Taoism has been extremely influential, and it embodies the concept that the human being has a potential for becoming an Immortal. That's why the belief spread that medicine fit for an Immortal could not be partaken of by ordinary mortals.

L.: But when ordinary people take Chinese medicine today, what do they take and what methods of cure do they follow?

I.: Modern science to the present time is unclear as to the significance of Chinese medicine. Pharmacology, for example, has tended to analyze individual herbs and to strive to ascertain a definite structural formula. However, Eastern medicine cannot be comprehended through this method.

L.: Why can't it be comprehended? Can't it be analyzed?

I.: The area that defies analysis is regarded as mysterious, but it really isn't. In other words, analysis shows the chemical make-up of a substance but this is not relevant to Eastern considerations. For

---

* The translation of an impromptu taped discussion in Japanese, in which Dr. Ishihara answered at length on questions pertaining to his field of specialization. The tape, made in the late summer of 1968, was transcribed in October.

example, if 200 grams of beafsteak are eaten, one person will digest it completely while a second person with a weak constitution may be able to absorb only 50 of the 200 grams. In such a case, even though the same amount is eaten the efficacy attained by the person with the bad stomach is only one-fourth that of the healthy person. This is the factor that modern Western medicine tends to ignore.

L.: Are you saying, then, that the West tends to neglect the human factor?

I.: Yes, the totality of the human organism is forgotten. To give an illustration, modern dietetics operates on the thesis that the number of calories of food eaten daily are completely absorbed by each individual. But this isn't so for the person with a weak stomach. That's where the problem lies; however, the East doesn't follow this line of thinking, stressing as it does individual differences.

L.: For the average person, how would you define the principal area of difference between Chinese and Western medicine?

I.: Chinese medical prescriptions arose in China more than 2,000 years ago, unrelated to the kind of Western data in which results are achieved through animal experimentation. In modern medicine, the names of illnesses are precisely affixed and illnesses like cancer, neurosis and hysteria are considered incurable. European medicine arose with animals as the object of investigation. For example, there was the belief that cures for cats and dogs could be applied with equal validity to humans, since in all cases the bacteria were identical. However, cats and dogs don't suffer from neuroses, so this disease was very hard to cure. On the other hand Oriental medicine is unrelated to the designations of illnesses current in Western medicine. Another factor is that Chinese medicines are all composed of natural ingredients.

L.: Is that true in every case?

I.: Yes, it is. We humans grow from birth onwards through eating natural things. Our bodies therefore are accustomed to distinguishing the components of what we eat, taking in only what is necessary. But sometimes the body rejects the strong modern medicines that are made up of chemical substances. The most conspicuous example of this occurs when the body reacts adversely to a chemical drug. Since Chinese drugs are natural, if the body does reject them it does so through vomiting or diarrhea, without further reaction. But in modern medicine the adverse reaction to injections is much more violent.

L.: Why is that so?

I.: The injection goes directly into the bloodstream, and the result may be a worsening of the human condition.

L.: Do Chinese medicines have to be taken over a long period in order to achieve effect? Is Western medicine quicker in getting the desired results?

I.: It's quicker, but all it does is temporarily alleviate the manifestations of illness such as fever or pain, without producing a fundamental cure. Pain-killing drugs, for example, kill the pain but they fail to effect a cure, and later the pain reoccurs.

L.: What method does Chinese medicine adopt?

I.: Through its medicines it changes the constitution of the patient, bringing about a fundamental cure. It divides humans into four basic types:
First there is the spirit-stagnant person, whose pent-up grievances lead to illness. This type suffers from neurosis and, if a female, contracts hysteria. These persons have blocked feelings, which have to be liberated through the use of medicines such as odoriferous herbs. There is an analogy to this practice in ancient Rome and Greece, where amomile and angelica were used. These are still resorted to in French villages and in the Alps.

L.: How about the second type?

I.: The second type is one whose blood becomes poisoned. This concept is completely lacking in Western medicine, but in Japan since olden times it has been referred to as a malady of old blood. Women in this category suffer from climacteric disease, and they are very numerous. Pregnant women who, not wanting children, have abortions come to contract this malady of the blood. Other women fail to recover fully from childbirth.

L.: Do they suffer from gynaecology?

I.: Yes, they do. But men come under this category as well, like those with hemorrhoids whose blood gets stopped up. In Japan, this illness gave rise to a play on words, since the words for "old blood " (*oketsu*) and " anus " (*oketsu*) had the same pronunciation. The third type is called " water poison ", referring in modern medical terms to the kidney disease of edema, also called nephritis. Chinese medical concepts deal with the poisons of air, blood, and water.

The fourth type, identified not by Chinese but by native Japanese medical concepts, is the poison that results from eating unnatural foods. To the Chinese physician, ideal foods are identified with the five elements of wood, fire, earth, metal, and water. There are five flavors: sour (wood), bitter (fire), sweet (earth), peppery (metal), and salty (earth), and they all have to be harmonized.

L.: When one gets sick in the West, he goes to the doctor and takes blood tests, gets ex-rayed, etc. However, a couple of months ago when my wife wasn't feeling well you simply observed her facial color and remarked that she had stomach trouble. And that was actually so. How does the Chinese physician arrive at a diagnosis, simply through looking at the patient's skin?

I.: No, through observing facial color, eyes and skin, and through taking the pulse.

L.: Did you learn these things in medical school?

I.: Chinese theories of the five elements and such are philosophical but not scientific. We practitioners of Chinese medicine in Japan apply the ancient concepts where we understand them, but where we do not we resort to Western tests and medical techniques. The ancient concepts deal with significance of facial color, eyes, skin, and pulse.

Western and Eastern medicine differ fundamentally in one respect. The West relies on statistical data, the East on the doctor's intuition. Eastern medicine is synonymous with the physician's art. In the Han history written by Ssu-ma Ch'ien*, physicians were divided into three types. The greatest of these could diagnose from facial color alone; the next in excellence could diagnose from the pulse, having to touch the person; but the least skilled of all had to ask in detail about the patient's condition in order to discover what ailed him.

---

* See *Shih-chi* 史記, biographies of Pien Chi 扁鵲 and Ts'ang Kung 倉公.

L.: To what extent can we rely on the statements about medicine in the 28th section of *Ishimpō* that we have just translated?

I.: I have translated the text with you, but as yet I haven't had a chance personally to check the prescriptions. I understand that someone in Japan who had read the text had some of the prescriptions prepared by a local druggist, especially the one called Bald Hen Potion.

L.: What was the result of the Bald Hen Potion? Was it efficacious?

I.: I understand that it was first made into a powder, then put into a capsule form, and sold. It sold very well; the general reaction of the purchasers was that it made them so ravenously hungry that they had to eat at once. Food converted into energy in this way would make the person more energetic, better prepared for sex activities.

L.: Wasn't Bald Hen Potion one of the aphrodisiacs mentioned in *Ishimpō*?

I.: Yes, it was. In Japan, one consumer said that his wife complained because she could not put up with his sexual exuberance. Others, however, said that it was totally ineffective. There might have been psychological reasons behind the reactions, one way or the other. The Bald Hen prescription had nothing in it one could call a direct sexual stimulant.

L.: Does this mean in an extended context that a person suffering from impotence might be impotent because of psychological rather than physiological reasons?

I.: Because of the psychological factor, those who believe in a prescription may feel that it works for them, while those who don't believe in it will feel the opposite way. This same psychological factor was operative not only in China, but in ancient Greece and Rome as well. The Roman physician Dioscorides, living in the time of Nero (ca. 60 B.C.), prescribed many things in his *Materia Medica* whose effects depended on the patient's psychology. Many of those prescriptions resembled those used in Chinese medicine.

L.: What happened afterwards?

I.: To the present day peasants in Portugal, Spain and France still use some of his prescriptions, though none of them are medically prescribed. They are all based on natural ingredients.

L.: On the subject of aphrodisiacs, how about the use of deer's horn?

Was this popular because the shape of the horn resembled that of the penis?

I : In China (and in Europe as well), there was the homeopathic belief that one thing similar to another could bring about a cure   This is really a superstition, but it represents the origin of medicines.

L.: Is there anything special about the way deer horn is constituted?

I.: Young deer horn especially is filled with hormones.   Experiments with mice have shown that mice who take this become much more sexually potent.

L.: Is this a recent experiment?

I.: It was performed in the Soviet Union at the start of the century. The best young deer horns are those found on reindeer in Northeast China and Siberia; Japanese deer horn is not at all efficacious.   The large deer horn is of no use, the small horn (which looks like the penis) the best.

L.: What kind of deer are alluded to in *Ishimpō*?

I.: Not the Japanese deer, but probably deer imported into Japan from T'ang China.

L.: Is deer horn still used today as an aphrodisiac?

I.: Yes, in the Orient of course, and also in Mexico and among Eskimos in Canada.   It's also used in the Soviet Union, Norway, and Sweden.

L.: Do modern doctors prescribe this for impotence?

I.: Physicians don't but it's popular among peasants, for example, who have heard about it from their parents or grandparents.

L.: Are there other medicines mentioned in *Ishimpō* which, like deer's horn, are still very popular today?

I.: Yes, the salted pulpy mushroom variety (肉蓯蓉) not available in Japan.   The Japanese equivalent is considered to be a yellowish-purple mushroom (黄紫茸) found in high mountains like Mount Fuji or in the Japan Alps.   However, it has no effect at all.   The salted pulpy mushroom has some manganese in it, and this is believed to contain the qualities of an aphrodisiac.   It's still found on the Chinese mainland, in Szechwan and Yunnan.

L.: How about Korean ginseng?

I.: It is mentioned only once in *Ishimpō*.

L.: Westerners very often hear about this.   Are there many varieties of ginseng? How about its effect?

I.: Ginseng is also written in such a way as to refer to its having a human form (人蔘), and perhaps a belief in it developed because of its outer appearance.

L.: Did this start in Korea?

I.: No, it started in China, about 2,000 years ago. The best variety is in Manchuria, the next best in North Korea. During their occupation of Korea, the Japanese encouraged its production, and it became a Japanese government monopoly. The larger ginseng is the better it is—the Southern Korean variety is small. The old and large natural varieties from Manchuria and North Korea may sell for as high as one to two million yen each. I saw one like this on sale in Hong Kong for two million yen.

L.: Why is ginseng inserted in alcohol, as in Seoul?

I.: Because it absorbs very well the qualities of the ginseng.

L.: What's the best way to use ginseng?

I.: It is best used by those who are weak and run-down.

L.: There are references in *Ishimpō* to enlarging the penis; I've noted that Orientals are very conscious of this factor of size. I read recently an ad in the Japan Times for an operation to enlarge the penis. The Chinese novel *Jou-p'u t'uan* (" Prayer-Mat of Flesh ") cites an operation of this kind in which a dog's penis was grafted on. Is the penis-enlargement operation world-wide, or is it restricted to Japan?

I.: This operation is relatively recent, dating back about fifty years. At present, circumcision is becoming more popular with the Japanese male. From a sexual standpoint, it is better not to do this, for when the foreskin is unsheathed it sharpens the male reaction. The prescriptions in *Ishimpō* about enlarging the penis by one or two inches are exaggerated.

L.: Are the prescriptions at all efficacious?

I.: The ingredients stimulate the penis, which therefore becomes enlarged—the effect is like sprinkling a pepper-like substance on it.

L.: Viewing the section in *Ishimpō* on the largeness of the jade gate, it seems of interest that more than a thousand years ago this worried the married couple.

I.: It's worth noting that sulphur was prescribed for size reduction, but I don't know if it actually had such an effect. According to *Ishimpō*, the fumes from the sulphur were to be added to the jade gate.

L.: Was there a danger in this, as alleged in *Ishimpō*?

I.: I don't think so. The effect of these prescriptions seems to have been exaggerated.

L.: Were such statements based on superstition?

I.: Perhaps half and half, the other half in the realm of faith.

L.: How about stopping the woman's pain from the first intercourse?

I.: The medicines in *Ishimpō* for this were efficacious. For example, cuttlefish bones when ground into a powder are effective in stopping bleeding and in alleviating pain.

L.: Weren't some superstitions injected, like burning hair to make a powder to place on the wound?

I.: This is still used—I've used it myself. It works to stop the bleeding instantly. The pure carbon from the bottom of a pot could also be used to stop the bleeding. Tamba Yasuyori probably experimented with ingredients whose validity he doubted.

L.: To appreciate the significance of *Ishimpō* for its times, one should bear in mind that it was intended for use by the aristocracy.

I.: Westerners who want to experiment with the prescriptions in *Ishimpō* will find this difficult to do, because many of the ingredients are available only in China or in the East.

Three: Levy-Ishihara Dialogue on Acupuncture*

Levy: When foreigners think of acupuncture, they usually regard it as something frightening and very primitive. For the elucidation of the West, would you care to expound briefly at this time on the history and significance of acupuncture?

Ishihara: The art of acupuncture is extremely old, dating back more than 5,000 years. It originated by the upper reaches of the Yellow River as a folk medicine of the Chinese. The peoples of this region led a nomadic existence, moving with their sheep and other animals from one oasis to another. The variety of foods was severely limited-even today there are said to be only seven kinds of Mongolian foods. Few were the herbs, therefore, that could be used for medical purposes, and the treatment and cure of illness presented a serious problem. There were climatic extremes of heat and cold, and the most pressing question for a member of the nomadic group was that of losing the ability to walk—this was tantamount to suffering the fate of abandonment and death.

When pain and a benumbing loss of sensation resulted in a failure of locomotion, the need arose for an effective and reliable method of treatment to bring about an instant cure, irrespective of time or place. Acupuncture and moxibustion came into being as a consequence.

L.: You mention acupuncture and moxibustion, but I think that the average Westerner is unable to distinguish one from the other.

I.: In acupuncture, a needle made of gold, silver, or iron is inserted, but in moxibustion fire is applied to the cap of a needle, the cap being covered by mugwort. Heat may also be applied directly to the skin, by burning mugwort on it. Modern needles may also be made from platinum and cobalt. Sometimes it becomes difficult to differentiate precisely between these two modes of treatment, which in Eastern medical thought are considered as part of

---

* Also conducted in Japanese and recorded on tape in the late summer of 1968, and then transcribed and translated.

the same process.

L.: Westrrners regard them as two completely different things. They believe that the insertion of a needle into the body must be very painful, probably because they associate it with the pain of inoculations.

I.: Not only Westerners, but many modern Japanese as well react to acupuncture in that way. The reason is that the word " needle " conjures up terms like sewing needles and the needles used in inoculations. But such thick needles are never used—acupuncture needles are extremely slender. The needle that causes pain through insertion can never be effective in stopping pain. An acupuncture needle applied effectively in the appropriate place is painless.

L.: Can the needle be applied in the same place, irrespective of who the patient is, without drawing blood?

I.: This is a very complex question. For example, there is a chart showing the places on the body where a needle can be inserted, but these are not absolute and fixed position designators. The size indicators on the chart refer to the right thumb size of the male and the left thumb size of the female. The upper line that crosses the thumb at the first joint is considered a " one-inch " measurement, belonging to that person alone. Another " one-inch " measurement in Chinese medical terms is the area from the first to second joints of the index finger when it is in a bent position.

L.: Is this always successful? Does the needle ever draw blood?

I.: No, never. The personal measurement accords exactly with each person's physical size, so there is no room for error in estimating position based on this scale. Furthermore, the physician doesn't insert the needle mechanically, but instead he probes with his finger to ascertain the place where the reaction is greatest—that is where he makes the insertion. The patient's skin reacts in varied ways to the press of the finger, including pain or pleasure, softness or hardness to the touch. The reaction depends on the person and on the type of illness being treated. In turn it determines the manner of insertion, strong or weak. In some cases the needle is not inserted at all but instead it merely grazes the skin. Skin-grazing has the same effect as massage.

This is very hard for Westerners to understand, but in Chinese medical thought a human being's life energy is divided into female and male (*yin-yang*) elements. These elements flow within the body according to a fixed pattern, and the needle is inserted at a place where life energy enters and exits.** Life energy follows a certain route*** as it flows from one place to the next. These are the curative points, as considered by acupuncture. To phrase this briefly, the medical technique of acupuncture is to trace the cause of all illnesses to deviations in the route of life energy. Having done this, the decision is then made whether to insert a needle or to apply moxibustion to that point which provides the greatest reaction.

L.: What is the percentage of success as compared with modern medicine? Is acupuncture used to cure illnesses considered incurable in the West? Is is used to effect cures without going through the necessity of an operation? When and for what kinds of ailments is it best to use acupuncture?

I.: It is extremely effective for sudden emergencies involving extreme pain and paralysis in cases of rheumatism and neuralgia—in other words, as a physical therapy which obviates the use of drugs such as morphine.

L.: If it is so successful, why isn't acupuncture more widely practiced throughout Japan? Like Chinese medicine, is its practice restricted only to those who possess a physician's qualifications?

I.: Modern Japanese doctors study neither Chinese medicine nor acupuncture as a part of the academic curriculum. Medical schools in Japan are all based on Western medicine alone—this statement applies to our forty-six medical colleges. Traditional medicine is excluded from the Japanese curriculum.

L.: I understand that acupuncture is now being practiced in France and Germany, but what is the reason for this and how did it begin?

I.: Two years ago, in the autumn of 1966, an International Congress

---

** The exact place is a technical term in Chinese acupuncture called *ching-k'ung* 經穴 in Chinese, *tsubo* in Japanese. There is no precise English term to render this expression, which pertains to the "curative points" for acupuncture and moxibustion.

*** This route is called *ching-lo* 經絡 in Chinese, *keiraku* in Japanese.

of Acupuncture and Moxibustion was held in Tokyo. I attended, and was impressed by the fact that there were many certified physicians in attendance. They came from more than ten nations such as France, Germany, the United States, Canada, and Argentina. But there were very few Japanese physicians at the Congress. Japanese acupuncturists are not physicians—they receive a special license, somewhat like chiropractors in the United States.

The Japanese acupuncturist is generally unfamiliar with Western medicine or the modern scientific approach, and therefore he will try to cure a disease like cancer even when in the West it might normally be considered incurable. There is a real problem here concerning the extent to which cancer is curable through resorting to acupuncture or Chinese medicine, but there have been examples of cures.

L.: About how many acupuncturists are there in Japan? For example, in our earlier dialogue I believe you said that less than one hundred licensed physicians are licensed to practice Chinese medicine, out of a total of 120,000 Japanese doctors.

I.: In Japan today there are probably only about fifty certified physicians like myself who are qualified to practice acupuncture. And about fifteen persons out of this group are qualified to practice Western medicine, Chinese medicine, and acupuncture.

L.: How about the status of those who practice only acupuncture?

I.: There are about 120,000 " pre-doctors " in Japan who have special licenses to practice massage and/or moxibustion and acupuncture. However, massage and moxibustion predominate because these are much easier to master—acupuncture techniques are complex and difficult to understand. These " pre-doctors " are forbidden to dispense medicines, and what they do is limited to physical therapy.

L.: Is there any difference in pre-war and post-war Japanese attitudes towards acupuncture?

I.: Yes, a marked difference. Before the second World War, old people in the village had a superstitious faith in acupuncture, but from 1945 onwards interest in Chinese medicine and acupuncture among young intellectuals noticeably increased.

L.: Does the effect of acupuncture vary widely from one individual to another?

I.: Yes, it does. For example, in the case of rheumatism, this is the name of an illness as affixed by modern medicine. This varies, however, from person to person. Acupuncturists disregard the name of the illness and inspect the pulse. They concentrate on discovering the curative points at which the needle can be affixed with best effect. Oriental medicine looks at the individual, and acts accordingly. It can never depend for its diagnosis on a description from a third party.

The West regards massage, acupuncture, and moxibustion in different ways, but to the East they are similar in aspect, for the objective is to relate treatment to a specific individual. What works for one person doesn't necessarily work for another.

L.: What is the current situation among the Chinese? To what extent do they still practice acupuncture?

I.: It flourishes both in Taiwan and on the mainland, with a pragmatic emphasis on using its efficacious aspects. It is looked upon as a precious part of China's cultural heritage.

L.: How do you regard the future of acupuncture and its reception in both East and West during the next fifty years?

I.: Even in Japan today, general clinics for the treatment of pain have been established which avoid analysis of specific ailments. Here the pain-alleviation effects of acupuncture are being studied. The centers for these studies are in Osaka and Kyoto Universities. In France and Germany, the first interest may have been in the mystic aspects of acupuncture, but afterwards the commercially rewarding use of acupuncture as an effective pain-killer was also studied. But now a movement has gotten under way which stresses the scholarly approach above all others.

L.: Changing the subject, there are a few references to acupuncture in *Ishimpō*, such as avoiding it during pregnancy. Why is this? And does acupuncture act as a sexual stimulant?

I.: Acupuncture is able to excite or depress the patient's sexuality, depending on the nature of the needle's vibrations. In the case of pregnancy, acupuncture can have a very adverse effect. In Eastern terms, acupuncture can cause an abortion through certain vibrations, affecting the incomplete fetus at a time when its life energy is still in a state of flux. But once the life energy is in harmony, as in the case of an adult, proper vibrations can elevate sexual awareness.

ANNOTATED BIBLIOGRAPHY
SELECTED BOOKS AND ARTICLES OF SINO-JAPANESE
SEXOLOGICAL IMPORT

Annotated Bibliography
Selected Books and Articles of Sino-Japanese Sexological Import

Introductory Remarks

This annotated bibllography, which has been developed by the co-translators in Yokohama, Japan, is intended primarily for the scholar interested in aspects of sexology who reads either Chinese or Japanese with facility. We have arranged relevant books and articles in chronological order, hoping to facilitate future researches by making sources to references quickly available. We have commented where direct knowledge or descriptive information was available. Lacking such information, we thought it best to list the reference without comment. Starred items refer to those works which we consider indispensable, usually because of a wealth of bibliographical information contained therein.

This first bibliographical effort is limited to about 250 citations (165 for China, 85 for Japan), arranged by chronological order and alphabetically by author within that order. The fact that we have done our work in Japan is readily apparent by the nature of our contribution, whose originality lies mainly in uncovering little-known Japanese sources. For things Chinese, we are heavily indebted to the original researches of the late R. H. van Gulik, the great sinologist who was the first scholar in the West to explore Chinese sexological books in depth. (In this regard, *Sexual Life in Ancient China* is a major twentieth-century contribution to our understanding of Chinese sex and society.)

There is a secretive aura that shields Oriental erotica from public view. Chinese authorities in the Ch'ing dynasty and their counterparts in the Tokunaga government forbade certain books which they considered injurious to the preservation of social mores, of which erotic writings formed a major part. These prohibitions encouraged private printings and discreet, not-for-sale distribution from friend to friend. As a consequence, there are many specimens of erotica unknown to the West and little known in the East, kept from dissemination and shielded from outside inquiry. (One Japanese scholar, Mr. Hayashi Toshikazu, has seen and listed more than 3,000 items of erotica from the Yedo (Tokugawa) era alone, almost all in private collections.) The bibliographer therefore can proceed with the assurance that his results will inevitably fall far short of being definitive, but that patience and persistence will be awarded by the discovery of materials cited in none of the great bibliographical references and unknown to the librarians of major Sino-Japanese collections. It is our optimistic hope that our book " The Tao of Sex " will be reprinted many times in future years. With each reprint, we plan to annotate an additional bibliography of 200 books and articles, hoping to conclude our study with about a thousand listings in all. Our efforts will be amply rewarded if they contribute to making sexological works more accessible to qualified researchers and help to create an atmosphere conducive to scholarly studies of Oriental sex mores and practices. Sinologists and Japanologists East and West tend to be a conservative group, to whom sex is often virtually taboo. They either ignore it totally in their studies of Sino-Japanese civilizations or regard it not as a central activity but as a trivial matter to be buried in a minor footnote. May this attitude change in the coming decades, and may colleagues who share our views on the necessity of sexological researches come forth and make their voices heard and their views known. And may Confucian-minded Orientalists accept the necessity of studying sex in order to understand more fully Asian societies past and present, just as anti-communists, for example, have recognized the fact that Chinese communism cannot be fully understood without a scholarly investigation of Maxist theory.

Errors in listings and descriptions, if brought to our attention, will be gratefully acknowledged and corrected in the second edition.

REFERENCES

A. China

I. GENERAL

Anonymous. *Tuan-hsiu pien* 斷袖篇. *Hsiang-yen ts'ung-shu* 香艷叢書 (abbreviated *HYTS*), vol. 9, ch. 2, fol. 1a–22a. (See General: *Hsiang-yen ts'ung-shu.*) A description of famous homosexuals of dynastic eras; apparently the only Chinese treatise of its kind. (see van Gulik, *op. cit.*, 63n.)

Caufeynon, Docteur, *L'Eunichisme: Histoire générale de la Castration.* Charles Offenstadt, Paris, undated (ca. 1890?).
Examines male and female castration in different societies and its effects, touching on (42–4) its history in China and the role it played in Chinese court life.

* Ch'en Tung-yüan 陳東原. *Chung-kuo fu-nü sheng-huo shih* 中國婦女生活史. Commercial Press, Shanghai, 1937.
A very valuable one-volume work, in which the author gives a history of Chinese women from earliest recorded times until the time of publication. He writes in a clear colloquial style, cites the original texts, and is exact in his citations. An indispensable reference.

Commissioners' Report. *Contagious Diseases Ordinance, Hong Kong.* House of Commons, 1880.
Much information on law cases involving unlicensed brothels in Hong Kong, with reference to ordinances, medical examinations, control, and arrests.

* Franke, Herbert, lengthy review article of R. H. van Gulik's *Erotic Colour Prints of the Ming Period*, ZDMG (Zeitschrift der Deutchen Morgenland-isches Gesellschaft), NF (Neue Folge) 30, 1955, 380–87.
A detailed essay which, while reviewing van Gulik's work in depth, gives an outline history of the development of erotica in China and Japan, citing many important references. This article is highly recommended, especially for those who want a quick and authoritative introduction to the field of Sino-Japanese sexology.

193

Gichner, Lawrence E. *Erotic Aspects of Chinese Culture.* Washington, D. C., 1957, privately printed, illustrated.
A work whose primary value is in the illustrations it contains, many of which would otherwise be extremely difficult to secure or examine.

Hayashi Fusao 林房雄. *Chūgoku senya ichiya* 中國千夜一夜. Kawade shobō 河出書房, Tokyo, 2 vols, black-and-white and color illustrations.
More than two hundred stories arranged according to season and theme, taken from Chinese dynastic histories and belles-lettres. The compiler introduces and concludes each tale, drawing from an extensive knowledge of traditional Chinese history. He elaborates on incidents and effectively enlivens the original materials.

* *Hsiang-yen ts'ung-shu* 香艷叢書 (Abbreviated *HYTS*), ("*A Collection of Feminine Fragrance*"). *Kuo-hsüeh fu-lun she* 國學扶輪社, Shanghai, 1908–1910, 10 vols., about 120 folios in each volume.
A voluminous collection of essays and stories about Chinese women, covering a wide expanse of time. The contents generally combine literary embellishments with hints at sexual dalliance. (For examples in translation, cf. *The Illusory Flame* and *Warm-Soft Village.*)

* Iwai Hirosato, "*The Buddhist Priest and the Ceremony of Attaining Womanhood during the Yuan Dynasty*," Memoirs of the Research Department of The Toyo Bunko (The Oriental Library), Tokyo, No. 7, 1935, 105–61.
A learned article, thoroughly researched and admirably presented, on the practice of defloration among non-Chinese tribes from the T'ang to modern times. The writer concludes that it was a solemn religious ceremony, without erotic significance. Many Eastern and Western sources are summarized and/or translated.

* Karsch-Haack, F. *Forschungen über gleichgeschlecht liche Liebe.* Verlags buchhandlung Seitz & Schauer. München, 1906 foreword; undated. A history of homosexuality in China, Japan and Korea, with the emphasis on modern times. Detailed and well researched.

Kawakatsu Yoshio 川勝義雄, tr. H. Maspero's "*Le Taoisme*", entitled *Dōkyō* 道教. Tōkai Daigaku shuppankai 東海大学出版会, Tokyo, 1966.
A translation of the French monograph, with two important elements added. Occasional errors in the French translations of texts are corrected, and the original texts alluded to in the monograph are supplied in full in the section on notes.

Laufer, Berthold, "*Comments on Hermaphroditism*," American Journal of Physical Anthropology 3 (1920), 259–62.

Herbert Franke, review article, ZDMG, 1955, 386, cites this reference by Laufer, which we have not seen.

Levy, Howard S. *The Illusory Flame*, Kenkyusha, Tokyo, 1962, illustrated.
Ten translations of stories about women in love, taken from the Chinese collection on love and related subjects called *Hsiang-yen ts'ung-shu* 香艶叢書 ("A Collection of Feminine Fragrance "), q.v. The stories range in time from the fourteenth to nineteenth centuries.

Levy, Howard S. *Warm-Soft Village*, Dai Nippon Insatsu, Tokyo, 1964, illustrated.
Essays from Chinese and Japanese sources on marital relations and illicit love, mainly written in Ming and Ch'ing, which conclude with a series of sketches about profligate Buddhist nuns. The ten translations are annotated.

Liang Kuo-cheng 梁國正. *Wen-jo-hsiang chi* 温柔鄉記. In HYTS, vol. 9, fol. 17a–21b.
An ingenious description of woman in terms of the geographic features encountered in and around " Warm-Soft Village ", a metaphor for a woman's sexual charms. Many Taoist sex terms are cited (Cf. van Gulik, *Sexual Life . . .*, 283n).

* Ling-yün ko-chu 凌雲閣主 (pseudonym). *Li-tai ti-wang hsing-ai mi-wen* 歷代帝王性愛秘聞. Ta-t'ung shu-chü 大同書局, Tainan, 1959.
There are more than one hundred essays on sexual aspects of palace and harem life, brief but information-filled and persuasive. Interspersed throughout the essays are many quotations from primary sources which, however, are not precisely indicated.

* Maspero, Henri, " *Les Procédés de " Nourrir Le Principe Vital " dans La Religion Taoiste Ancienne*," Journal Asiatique 229, Paris, Apr.–June and July-Sept., 1937, 177–252, 353–430.
Two detailed and learned articles on Taoist conservation practices, describing essential sexual aspects such as " making the semen return " 還精. This superb study is replete with citations and translations from a wealth of primary Chinese sources.

Maspero, Henri. *Le Taoisme, II*. (Mélanges posthumes sur les religions et l'histoire de la Chine.) Civilizations du sud, Paris, 1950.
A masterful analysis of Taoist philosophical and religious practices, which includes a discussion of sexual practices (cf. 114–15).

Mitamura Taisuke 三田村泰助. *Kangan* 宦官. Chūō kōronsha, 中央公論社, Chūkō shinsho 中公新書 series, vol. 7, Tokyo, 1963.
A comprehensive monograph which traces the development of the eunuch

system in China from its origins in the Spring and Autumn period through the Ch'ing dynasty. It cites many sources, and is a first-rate scholarly study. It has scattered references to eunuch-consort and eunuch-sovereign love relations, relatively detailed for the Ming, when eunuchs in the harem were especially numerous.

Nagao Ryūzō 永尾龍造. *Shina minzokushi* 支那民俗誌. Shina minzokushi kankōkai, Tokyo, 1940, vol. 1.

Two pages (200–01) on religious New Year observances of Chinese prostitutes in Peking and Tientsin. An earlier work with the above title by this author, published in about 1919, had a chapter on the custom in Shantung of exhibiting stained bedsheets after the wedding night as proof that the bride was a virgin. I was shown the book five years ago, but have been unable to locate it since.

Needham, Joseph, with the research assistance of Wang Ling. *Science and Civilization in China:* vol. 2. History of Scientific Thought. The University Press, Cambridge, 1956.

This famed study has a very good general description of Taoist sexual practices (pp. 146–153), placing them within an overall philosophical-historical context. There are many valuable bibliographical references on these pages to extant and non-extant sources. At the time of writing, the fact that Yeh Teh-hui assembled his fragments of sex handbooks from *Ishimpō* 医心方 seems not to have been realized, for the connection between the two works, later made clear by van Gulik in *Sexual Life*, is not indicated. (It might also be erroneously inferred from the Needham study that *Ishimpō* was not " printed " (i.e., available for reading) until the nineteenth century.) The generalization that the Taoists accepted " the equality of women with men " (p. 151) is not borne out by the specific texts that we have translated. Our texts show that woman was manipulated and made to serve man's longevity-salvation objectives. (In only one chapter, the third, is there a reversal of roles, with woman instructed on how to take sexual advantage of unknowing young virgin males.)

* Okanishi Tameto 岡西為人 and others, ed. *Sung i-ch'ien i-chieh k'ao* 宋以前医籍考, Jen-min wei-sheng ch'u-pan she 人民衛生出版社. Peking, 1958, 491–97.

Dr. Okanishi was a professor at the medical school of Manshū University who, assisted by a group of Japanese co-workers, produced a handwritten manuscript consisting of the titles of thousands of pre-Sung Chinese works on medicine. The manuscript was expropriated by the Chinese communists in 1944, and published by them in Peking fourteen years later. Pages 491–97 list the titles of about eighty monographs on the bedroom arts, almost all of which are no longer extant, and show where monographs were originally cited.

Okuno Shintarō 奥野信太郎. *Chūgoku tsuya banashi* 中國艶ばなし. Bungei shunjū shinsha 文藝春秋新社, Tokyo, 1963, illustrated.

A personal, conversational approach to amorous Chinese stories, to which embellishments are added. Professor Okuno has a catholic knowledge of Chinese literature and customs, and many of his comments are original and contributive.

* K. Karol Pindor and others. *Report to the Council. Commission of Enquiry into Traffic in Women and Children in the East.* Series of League of Nations Publications (IV. Social), April 8, 1932 ; preface dated December 10, 1932.

This is an extremely detailed work, setting forth the results of an inquiry into international traffic in China, France, Japan, India, The Netherlands, Persia, Portugal, Siam, and The United Kingdom. All governments listed above authorized the inquiry, which cost less than $125,000 to conclude! The report states that the bulk of the traffic was in Asiatic women from one country of Asia to another, with Chinese and Japanese women (in that order) forming the preponderant majority. This is a key source for studying international aspects of prostitution, with the focus on Asia.

Schroder, Dominik, " *Bemerkungen zur Scheffel-zeremonie bei der Hochzeit der Tsinghai-Chinesen* ", *Anthropos* 51, 1956, 1089–96.

The writer includes two short discussions of defloration and the rights of the first night (*jus primae noctis*). Cf. General : Iwai.

Shibukawa Genji 澁川玄耳, *Shina keibō hishi* 支那閨房秘史. Hakueisha 白水社, Tokyo, 1928.

The author translates a few key sources such as *Lieh-nü chuan* 列女傳, relating to marital and harem behavior from Han to Ming times. Another edition was published in 1938 under the title, *Shina keibō hishi* 支那閨房秘史.

Stent, G. Carter. *Chinesische Eunuchen.* Leipzig, Otto Schulze, undated (ca. 1880 ?).

An undated translation of Stent's work, apparently unauthorized. (See next item.)

Stent, G. Carter, " *Chinese Eunuchs,*" Journal of the North China Branch of the Royal Asiatic Society, vol. XI, 1877, 143–84.

A very important article on eunuchs, by an eye-witness who includes much information on late Ch'ing practices (165–82) and details on the actual operation (170–71).

T'ien-nan yeh-sou 天南野叟 (pseudonym). *Ssu-kung yen-shih* 四宮艷史. Shih-chieh shu-chü 世界書局, Shanghai, 1922, 4 vols., each vol. about forty folios.

Four volumes on amorous activities in the Han, Sui, T'ang and Ch'ing palaces, attributed to a compiler with the pseudonym of "An Uncultured Old Man of T'ien-nan." The stories are written in a balanced classical style, easy to comprehend, which combine literary elegance with detailed information on palace life. Complete monographs are provided on Sui Yang-ti, Wu Tse-t'ien, and Yang Kuei-fei, with much fictional material interspersed.

* van Gulik, R. H. *Sexual Life in Ancient China.* E. J. Brill, Leiden, 1961, illustrated.

The major study of our times on Chinese sexology, embodying the knowledge and insights of an eminent Western sinologist. The work abounds in original and discerning observations, based on extensive reading in primary sources and on long residence in China. Aspects of sexual life are presented in chronological order, from earliest recorded history to 1644 (the end of the Ming dynasty). See this monograph for bibliographical references to larger works that include brief but pertinent sexological comments.

Veith, Liza, tr. *Huang ti nei ching suwen: The Yellow emperor's classic of internal medicine ch.* 1–34. University of California Press, Berkeley, 1966.

* Dr. Woo Chan Cheng, *Érotologie de la Chine.* J. J. Pauvert, Paris, 1963, profusely illustrated; includes a brief bibliography.

" Dr. Woo Chan Cheng " was said to have been the pseudonym of a Chinese professor, who subsequently died in exile at Singapore. The work contains essays on philosophic concepts of eroticism and on erotic aspects in Chinese society, art and literature. It is of special value in making available many rare erotic Chinese paintings which, however, are at times somewhat unclear.

II. PRE-HAN

Granet, Marcel. *La Polygynie Sororale et le sororat dans la Chine Fèodale.* Editions Ernest Leroux, Paris, 1920.

Polygamy involving sisters, translations of relevant genealogical texts, and analysis of the social origins and structure of sororal polygamy as it existed in the Chou Dynasty.

Hentze, C., "*Le Poisson Comme Symbole de Fecondité dans la Chine Ancienne,*" Bulletin of the Royal Museum, Brussels, 1930.

III. HAN

Anonymous. *Chao Fei-yen wai-chuan* 趙飛燕外傳. In Ku-shih wen-fang hsiao-shuo 顧氏文房小説.
T'ang version of the Han love encounters of Emperor Ch'eng-ti with Flying Swallow Chao and her voluptuous sister, described in *Warm-Soft Village*, 20–6.

Ssu-ma Hsiang-ju 司馬相如. *Mei-jen fu* 美人賦. Tr. in G. Margoulies' *Anthologie raisonée de la Litterature chinoise*, Payot, Paris, 1948, 324–26.
van Gulik, *Sexual Life . . .*, 68–9, also translates this poetical essay, which he refers to as " one of the earliest examples of consciously-erotic prose."

Yang Shen 楊愼 (1488–1559). *Tsa-shih pi-hsin* 雜事必幸. In Han Wei ts'ung-shu pieh-shih 漢魏叢書別史.
Fictional acount of how a Han emperor had a woman chosen as his empress, with emphasis on inspection in the candidate's bedroom. van Gulik, *op. cit.*, 208, places the authorship in Ming and with Yang Shen. While the Han attribution is spurious, the erotic theme is skilfully expressed.

Yüan Mei 袁枚 (1716–1797). *K'ung-ho-chien chi* 控鶴監記. Edition not located.
A spurious erotic text, said to have been a T'ang work, which van Gulik assumes was written by Yüan Mei (*op. cit.*, 208).

IV. POST-HAN AND PRE-T'ANG

Ch'en Shao 陳劭. *T'ung-yu chi* 通幽記. In Chiu hsiao-shuo 舊小説, Commercial Press, V, 114. Partial tr. in *Roku-chō Tō Sō shōsetsushū* 六朝唐宋小説集, Heibonsha, 1962, 273–74, under *T'ung-yu lu* 通幽録.
Erotic practices alluded to in this fictional work are cited by Dr. Herbert Franke in his review article of van Gulik's *Erotic Colour Prints* (see General : Franke).

Feng Chih 馮贄. *Nan-pu yen-hua chi* 南部烟花記. In T'ang-tai ts'ung-shu 唐代叢書 (see under *T'ang*; abbreviated *TTTS*), vol. 5, ch. 47, fol. 29a–30b.
Stories about harem life and harem favorites in the Ch'en and Sui dynasties, with concentration on the activities of Sui Yang-ti.

Han Wu 韓偓. *Mi-lou chi* 迷樓記. In *TTTS*, vol. 5, ch. 43, fol. 17a–18a.
A brief account of the harem excesses of Sui Yang-ti at the " Maze Palace ", with emphasis on his later sexual indulgence.

Wright, Arthur F., " *Sui Yang-ti: Personality and Stereotype*," in *The Confucian Persuasion*, Stanford University Press, Stanford, 1960, 47–76.
Analysis (59–76) of the traditional portrayal of Sui Yang-ti as an evil and licentious ruler, showing how the characteristics of other " bad-last ruler " stereotypes were also attributed to the Sui sovereign.   The point is made in conclusion that Chinese Marxist writers have also repeated uncritically the bad-last ruler mythology.

Wu Yao-i 吳兆宜. *Yü-t'ai hsin-yung chien-chu* 玉台新詠箋註.   Sao-yeh-shan fang 掃葉山房 edition.
An annotated Ch'ing edition of a collection of poems dating from the Han to Liang dynasties, compiled by Hsü Ling 徐陵 (fl. end 6th c.).   Several poems of sexual significance are translated by van Gulik, *Sexual Life*, q.v.

Yeh Teh-hui (1864–1927), editor. *So-nü ching* 素女經 (*and Four Other Handbooks on Sex*).   In his compilation, Shuang-mei ching-an ts'ung-shu 雙梅景闇叢書, Shanghai, 1914 blockprint edition.

Yeh Teh-hui's reconstructions of five handbooks of sex as cited in the 28th section of *The Essence of Medical Prescriptions* (*Ishimpō* 医心方).   Four of these handbooks were mentioned in the *Sui History* (cf. van Gulik, *Sexual Life . . .*, 122–23, etal).

Yen Shih-ku. *Nan-pu yen-hua lu* 南部烟花録. *Shuo-fu* 説郛 edition.
A series of anecdotes about pre-T'ang emperors and harem favorites by an early T'ang editor.

V. T'ANG

Chang Pi 張必. *Chuang-lou chi* 粧樓記. *TTTS*, vol. 7, ch. 81, fol. 33b–36b.
A tenth century miscellany on feminine adornment which has varied comments on harem behavior and on what T'ang women did to beautify themselves.   (Cf. van Gulik, *op. cit.*, 189–90.)

Demiéville, Paul, " *La nouvelle mariée acariâtre*," Asia Major, New Series, London, vol. VII, 59–65.
Translation and discussion of a ballad about a wayward wife whose uninhibited ways of gadding about led to divorce, with reproduction of the manuscripts.   The language is described as being very vulgar and difficult to translate.

* Des Rotours, Robert. *Courtisanes Chinoises a la fin des T'ang entre circa 789 et le 8 janvier 881 : PEI-LI TCHE* (*Anecdotes du quartier du Nord*). Presses Universitaires de France, Paris, 1968.

This is the definitive study of *Pei-li chih* 北里志, copiously annotated and analyzed, with the original Chinese text from which the translation was made placed at the bottom of each page.   There is a wealth of information here on T'ang personages and texts, representing years of scholarly researches.   Professor Chen Tsu-lung was consulted on difficult translation problems.

Edwards, E. D. *Chinese Prose Literature*.   Probsthain, London, 1938, 2 vols; indices and bibliography.

A still useful analysis of the contents of the T'ang literary anthology *T'ang-tai ts'ung-shu*, in which many love stories were recorded.

Hsü Hsiao-t'ien 許嘯天.   *T'ang-kung erh-shih ch'ao yen-i* 唐宮二十朝演義. Hsin-hua shu-chü 新華書局, Shanghai, 1928.   1 volume of illustrations, 7 volumes of text; 100 stories, about 1500 pages.

The stories, which mainly elaborate on historical incidents affecting emperors and consorts, proceed chronologically from the end of the Sui and through the T'ang to the start of the Five Dynasties period.

* Kishibe Nario 岸辺成雄.   *Tōdai ongaku no rekishiteki kenkyū* 唐代音楽の 歴史的研究.   Tōdai daigaku shuppankai, Tokyo, 1961, 2 vols.

The second volume of this comprehensive monograph on T'ang music has much information about T'ang-Sung prostitution.

Kuhn, Franz, tr. *Po Hsing-chien's Die Schöne Li; Vom Totenhemd ins Brantkleid*. Insel-Verlag, Wiesbaden, 1959.

Translations of *Li-wa chuan* 李娃傳 and *Li Wu-shuang chuan* 李無雙傳. (Cf. Edwards, *Chinese Prose Literature*, vol. 2. 154–69, for a translation of the first T'ang tale, about a famous courtesan.)

Levy, Howard S., *The Gay Quarters of Ch'ang-an*, Orient/West, vol. 7, no. 9, Sept., 1962, 93–105.

An essay on Ch'ang-an prostitution and prostitutes, drawn from primary sources; annotated.

Levy, Howard S. *Harem Favorites of an Illustrious Celestial*.   Chung-t'ai Press, Taichung, 1958.   Extensive annotations from primary sources.

Study of the harem favorites of T'ang Hsüan-tsung 玄宗 (reigned 712–756), with historical consideration of his famed consort Yang Kuei-fei 楊貴妃. There are translations of the biographies of four consorts (from the T'ang standard histories) and of three unofficial documents.

Levy, Howard S., *Love Themes in T'ang Literature*, Orient/West, vol. 7, No. 1, Jan., 1962, 67–78.

An essay on T'ang love themes, which includes translations of erotic poems in *Yu-hsien k'u* 遊仙窟.

Levy, Howard S., *Record of the Gay Quarters*, Orient/West, vol. 8, no. 5, Sept.–Oct., 1963, 121–28; vol. 8, no. 6, Nov.–Dec., 1963, 115–22; vol. 9, no. 1, Jan.–Feb., 1964, 103–10.

An annotated translation in three installments of a late ninth-century reminiscence of gay quarter activities at Ch'ang-an, composed by an aging bureaucrat. There are many vignettes of T'ang courtesans and a detailed description of high-class houses of prostitution.

Levy, Howard S., *T'ang Courtesans, Ladies and Concubines*, Orient/West, vol. 7, no. 3, March, 1962, 49–64.

Translations of T'ang poems written by and about T'ang courtesans, mostly on love themes, and description of several women's manuals on correct behavior.

Levy, Howard S., " *T'ang Women of Pleasure*," Sinologica, vol. VIII, No. 2, 1965, 89–113.

An essay describing various types of T'ang prostitutes and entertainers, annotated and based on primary source materials.

Levy, Howard S., tr. Chang Wen-ch'eng's 張文戌 *Yu-hsien k'u* 遊仙窟 (" *The Dwelling of Playful Goddesses* "). Dai Nippon Insatsu, Tokyo, 1965, illustrated.

An annotated translation of a late seventh century Chinese novelette which describes through poetry and prose the love feelings of a young Chinese government official. It includes an annotated bibliography of ninety studies, mostly in Japanese, which are not duplicated in this bibliography.

Po Hsing-chien 白行簡 (died 826). *T'ien-ti yin-yang chiao-huan ta-lo-fu* 天地陰陽交歡大楽賦. Shuang-mei ching-an ts'ung-shu 雙梅景闇叢書. This poetical essay on the delights of intercourse, attributed to Po Hsing-chien, has been translated into Japanese in *Chūgoku seishi*. *Sojokyō* (see Republic: Nakayama), 242–53, and summarized in English and Latin by van Gulik, *op. cit.*, 203–7. As van Gulik remarks, the text is in bad condition. Without emendation, it would be extremely difficult to render in other than paraphrase.

Herbert Franke, review article, 2 DMG, 1955, 383, notes that Pelliot discovered the text in Tunhuang and Lo Chen-yü produced a facsimile of it in 1913 in *Tung-huang shih-shih i-shu*. 敦煌石室遺書. Yeh Teh-hui included this in his collection (cited above) in 1914, one year after Lo Chen-yü had made the facsimile.

Sun Ssu-mo 孫思邈 (died 682). *Ch'ien-chin fang* 千金方. Japanese reprint of 1604 Ming edition, in 93 chapters.

The extensive T'ang monograph on how to achieve a healthy sex life. (Cf.

van Gulik, *Sexual Life*, 193–97, for translations, Ishihara, *Ishimpō*, and Herbert Franke, review article (General: Franke), 382, for comments.)

Sun Wei 孫頠. *Shen-nü chuan* 神女傳. TTTS, vol. 9, ch. 118.
Mildly erotic stories combined with the supernatural. T'ang writer Sun Wei's " Biographies of Goddesses " link beauty with out-of this-world-liness. One story refers to the sex handbooks (van Gulik, *op. cit.*, 208–9).

Tai Fou 戴孚. *Kuang-i chi* 廣異記. In Chiu hsiao-shuo V, 203. Partial Japanese tr. in *Roku-chō Tō Sō shōsetsushū*, 317–324.
References to a woman who was wondrously skilled in the sexual arts as taught in the old handbooks. (Cf. Franke, review article of *Erotic Colour Prints*, ZDMG, 1955, 382.)

Tai Wang-shu, " *Notes sur le Li-wa-tchouan*," French Institute of Peking, Peking, 1951.
Published in Chinese, with an abstract in French, the article contains a map of the Gay Quarters (van Gulik, *op. cit.*, 171n.). For an English translation of this famous tale of a T'ang courtesan, cf. Edwards, *Chinese Prose Literature*, vol. 2, 154–69.

* *T'ang-tai ts'ung-shu* 唐代叢書. Shanghai, Min-chang t'u-shu chü 錦章圖書局, ca. 1927, 20 vols., 164 items.
A treasury of T'ang literature, with many accounts of mild erotic interest. Abbreviated *TTTS*.

Ts'ui Ling-ch'in 崔令欽, " *Chiao-fang chi* " 教坊記, TTTS, vol. 5, ch. 49, f. 32a–34a.
A valuable T'ang monograph on the organization of palace training centers for musicians and entertainers. Several hundred T'ang song-names are recorded.

Wang, Elizabeth Te-chen. *Ladies of the T'ang*. Taipei, Heritage Press, 1961, a few illustrations.
Translations of 22 stories attributed to the T'ang, all but one taken from the *T'ai-p'ing kuang-chi* 太平廣記. There is a general introduction on the development of *hsiao-shuo*, usually translated as " short stories." Most of the stories deal with man-woman relationships.

Yen Shih-ku 顏師古. *Ta-yeh shih-i chi* 大業拾遺記. In *Shuo-fu*, vol. 110.
An early T'ang account of the harem antics of Sui Yang-ti.

VI. FIVE DYNASTIES AND SUNG

Chou Mi 周密. *Wu-lin chiu-shih* 武林舊事. In Pao-yen-tang mi-chi kuang-han 宝顔堂秘笈廣函.

A description of life in the Southern Sung Capital of Hangchou, with sociological information on the organization of low and high class prostitution
(Cf. van Gulik, *op. cit.*, 230–33). The *Ssu-k'u t'i-yao* 四庫提要 editors
considered Chou Mi's statements to be reliable.

* Hsü Shih-lüan 徐士鸞. *Sung-yen* 宋豔盒. In Pi-chi hsiao-shuo ta-kuan
筆記小説大觀.

A voluminous compendium of primary and secondary Chinese sources
about maids, concubines and prostitutes in the Southern-Northern Sung
periods, divided into thirty-six subject categories. Sources are cited
throughout.

Levy, Howard S., *Chinese Footbinding: The History of a Curious Erotic
Custom.* Walton Rawls, New York, 1966, extensively illustrated.
A history of footbinding, with emphasis on esoteric-erotic aspects. Notes,
bibliography, and index.

Meng Yüan-lao 孟元老. *Tung-ching meng-hua lu* 東京夢華錄. Ku-tien
wen-hsüeh ch'u-she, Shanghai, 1956.
A collated edition of a work on Kaifeng, the capital of Northern Sung,
which includes a few essays about prostitution and prostitutes.

Nai-te-weng 尉得翁 (pseudonym). *Tu-ch'eng chi-sheng* 都城紀勝. In Wu-
lin chang-ku ts'ung-pien 武林掌故叢編, section 1.
Completed in 1235, this anonymous work presented miscellaneous facts
about Hangchou life, including information on low-class brothels and on
wine houses that provided prostitutes for its customers (van Gulik, *op.
cit.*, 231, 233).

Okamoto Ryūzō 岡本隆三. *Chūgoku no kishū* 中國の奇習. Kōbundō
弘文堂, Tokyo, 1965 ; a few illustrations.
This is the second edition of a work first published in 1963, under the title
of *Tensoku* 纏足 (" Footbinding "). It has some information on the erotic
appeal of the bound foot (58–79), considered within a social context of
dynastic palace life.

Tung-fang Shuo 東方脱 (pseudonym). *The Licentiousness of The Ardent
King of the Chin Kingdom*, Yokohama, Sino-Japanese Sexology Classics
Series, vol. III; scheduled for publication in 1969.
Introduction to and translation of a Sung story of the licentious behavior
of King Hai-ling of the Chin, killed while invading the Southern Sung
in 1161. The account, apparently written by an anti-Chin contemporary,
abounds in descriptions of harem behavior generally found in much later
writings. The original Chinese text is also being made available.

Wu Tzu-mu 呉子牧. *Meng Liang lu* 夢梁録. In Chih-pu tsu chai ts'ung-shu 知不足斉叢書, section 28.

Extensive collection of notes on Hangchou life, with references to marriage, concubinage and prostitution (Cf. van Gulik, op. cit., 234, 254). It was patterned after *Tung-ching meng-hua lu* 東京夢華録 ("A Record of the Dreamed-of-Splendors of the Eastern Capital").

Yao-Ling-hsi. *Ts'ai-fei hsin-pien* 采菲新編. Tientsin, T'ien-ching shu-chü, January, 1941; illustrated.

H. S. Levy refers to this book in the bibliography to *Chinese Footbinding* (p. 334), saying that perhaps it was not published. He was wrong; it was published, and he now has a copy of it.

Yao Ling-hsi 姚靈録. *Ts'ai-fei lu* 采菲録. Shih-tai kung-ssu 時代公司, Tientsin, reprinted Jan. 1, 1936; illustrated.

This was the first of five volumes of footbinding materials compiled by Yao Ling-hsi from 1936 to 1941. Each of the illustrated volumes contains about 300–360 pages of text, with many items of erotic interest scattered throughout. Cf. *Chinese Footbinding: The History of a Curious Erotic Custom*, for some of these erotic references and for bibliographical listings of other volumes on footbinding by Yao Ling-hsi. The bibliography in *Chinese Footbinding* cites many Chinese monographs that discuss aspects of footbinding and erotica.

VII. YÜAN

Bazin, M. *Le Pi-pa ki, ou Histore du Loth.* Paris, 1864.
A partial translation of a Yüan play (see Yüan: Hundhausen).

Gernet, Jacques. *La vie quotidienne En Chine á la veille de l'invasion mongole.* Hachette, Paris, 1959. See next citation for an English translation.

Gernet, Jacques (in translation). *Daily Life in China on the Eve of the Mongol Invasion* 1250–1276. London, 1962.
There is relevant information here on prostitution, including male prostitution, as it flourished in the big cities during the 13th century.

Hart, Henry H., tr. *The West Chamber.* Stanford University Press, Stanford, 1936.
A famous play of the Yüan period, about a love adventure of the T'ang poet Yüan Chen.

Hsia T'ing-chih 夏庭芝. *Ch'ing-lou chi* 青樓集. Chung-kuo wen-hsüeh t'an-k'ao tz'u-liao ts'ung-shu, Peking, vol. 8, 1957.

The biographies of famous prostitutes who lived towards the end of the Yüan dynasty. Character tends to be illustrated through anecdote. (Cf. Yüan: Waley.)

Hundhausen, V. tr., *Die Laute*. Peking, 1930.
Complete translation of a Yüan play about Han scholar Ts'ai Yung and his two principal wives.

Levy, Howard S., " *The Marvelous Mongolian; A T'ang Story*," Orient/ West, May, 1962, vol. 7, No. 5, 25–30.
Translation of a vivid account of the love adventures of a Mongol courtesan who flourished in early Ming times. (Later included in *The Illusory Flame*.) The story was erroneously sub-titled by the O/W editor.

Rudelsberger, Hans. *Altchinesische Liebes-Komöden*. Kunst verlag Anton Schroll & Co., Vienna, 1923; fine color and black-and-white illustrations. Abbreviated versions of five Yüan plays about love and courtesans. For the names of the plays, see van Gulik, *op. cit.*, 251n., who states that their texts supply good materials for studying sexual and social relationships.

T'ao Tsung-i 陶宗儀 (fl. 14th c.). *Yüan-shih yeh-t'ing chi* 元氏掖庭記. In Hsü Po-ch'uan hsüeh-hai 續百川學海, section B (ひ).
Description of Yüan harem life; it includes comments on Tantric sexual practices (van Gulik, *op. cit.*, 260 n.).

Waley, Arthur. *The Secret History of the Mongols, and Other Pieces*. Allen and Unwin, London, 1963.
The Yüan essay on prostitution called *Ch'ing-lou chi* 青樓集 is analyzed on pages 89–107, in an article called " *The Green Bower Collection*," which originally appeared in 1957 in *Oriental Art, New Series*.

VIII. MING

Acton, H., and Lee Yi-hsieh, tr. *Four Cautionary Tales*, London, 1947.
One of the four tales, " The Mandarin Duck Girdle," alleges that Ming nunneries were places where illicit love flourished.

Anonymous. *Chu-lin yeh-shih* 株林野史. Shanghai (reprint), ca. 1914.
The reprint of a Ming pornographic novel about orgies in a bamboo grove, based on a close reading of the ancient sex handbooks. The novel was placed on the index of forbidden books twice during the Ch'ing dynasty (Cf. van Gulik, *op. cit.*, 314–16).

Anonymous. *Ch'un-yang yen-cheng fou-yu-ti-chün chi-chi chen-ching* 純陽

演正孚祐帝君既濟眞經, Japan, blockprint edition, ca. 1880.
Brief text on Taoist sexual alchemy, which van Gulik (*op. cit.*, 278) believes dates from the early Ming period.

Anonymous late Ming Nanking literatus. *Chao-yang ch'ü-shih* 昭陽趣史 ; illustrations of erotic scenes.
• A novel combining elements of fox-love and sexual vampirism, described by van Gulik, *op. cit.*, 316–17.

Anonymous. *Su-nü miao-lun* 素女妙論. Collated blockprint edition, Japan, printed in 1536.
This edition contains, in red characters written alongside the printed text, another work on the bedroom arts called *Kuei-fang hsiu-yang* 閨房修養, which differs from *Su-nü miao-lun* slightly on minor points of phraseology. Both follow a Yellow Emperor-Woman Plain style. A Japanese translation of the *Su-nü* text was made by Manase Dōsan 曲直瀬道三 (1507–1594), a famed doctor of the Momoyama era, which he called *Kōso myōron* 黄素妙論 (Cf. van Gulik, *op. cit.*, 270–71). Dr. Ishihara believes that the *Su-nü* text probably dates back to Sung times and indicates a Chinese tradition independent of that in the twenty-eighth section of *Ishimpō*.

Buck, Samuel, tr. *Kwan Shan-mei's Don Juan of China, an amour from Chin P'ing Mei retold through text and pictures*. Tuttle, Tokyo and Vermont, 1960.

Chai-hung-lou chu-jen 摘紅樓主人 (pseudonym). *Su nü miao-lun* 素女妙論. Japanese manuscript copy, ca. 1880.
A Ming handbook of sex which has some content not found in the earlier sex bibles. Cf. van Gulik, *op. cit.*, 272–77, for translated extracts.

Egerton, Frank, tr. *The Golden Lotus (Chin P'ing Mei* 金瓶梅). London, 1955, 4 vols.
See van Gulik, *op. cit.*, 287–90, etal for a detailed description of the novel. Dr. van Gulik refers to Egerton's achievement as a " good English translation," but I should prefer to categorize it is a readable literary interpretation which does more than gentlemanly justice to the vulgarity of the orginal text. The translator's decorum, which resulted in his rendering erotic passages into Latin, may also have inhibited him from coming to grips with the vernacular tone of the Chinese text.

Etiemble, " *Jeou p'ou-touan ou Jeou pu-tuan?* " Nouvelle Revue Francaise n.s. 11, no. 121 (Jan., 1963), 108–13.

* Hanan, P. D., " *Sources of the Chin P'ing Mei*," Asia Major 10 (July, 1963), London, 23–67.

An article on identifying sources copied into the *Chin P'ing Mei*, citing original texts of surviving stories. The writer makes the important point that the novel was related to an earlier erotic tradition in Chinese fiction and traces its influence (43–7). Thoroughly researched and scientifically investigated.

* Hanan, P. D., " *The Text of the Chin P'ing Mei.*" Asia Major, London, new series 9 (April, 1962), 1–57.
A detailed study of editions and texts, including references to non-extant manuscripts. More than one hundred annotations, in which relevant sources are copiously cited.

Ingalls, Jeremy, " *Mr. Ch'ing-yin and the Chinese Erotic Novel,*" Yearbook of Comparative and General Literature, 13 (1964), 60–3.
An article about *Jou p'u t'uan.*

Inoue Kōbai 井上紅梅, tr. *Kin Pei Bai: Shina no shakai jotai* 金瓶梅: 支那の社会状態. Nihondō shoten 日本堂書店, Shanghai, 1923, 3 vols.
A Japanese translation of the erotic Ming Novel, with a chapter-by-chapter analysis of expressions in the original that are difficult to understand.

Dr. Keizo Dohi. *Beitrage zur Geschichte Der Syphillis, insbesondere über ihren Ursprung und ihre Pathologie in Ostasien.* Verlag von Nankodo, Tokyo, 1923.
A general discussion of medical treatises in China and Japan, followed by a description of how venereal disease spread in China in Ming times and appeared in Japan in the mid-sixteenth century.

Kuhn, Dr. Franz, tr. Li Yü's *Jou pu tuan.* Verlag Die Waage, Zurich, 1959.

Kuhn, Franz, tr. Li Yü's *Jou pu tuan.* Verlag die Waage, Hamburg, 1965, illustrated.

Levy, Howard S., tr. Yü Huai 于懷. *A Feast of Mist and Flowers (Pan-ch'iao tsa-chi* 板橋雜記), privately mimeographed, Yokohama, 1967; illustrated.
An annotated translation of a late Ming reminiscence of gay quarter activities in Nanking, preceded by the translator's essay on the Nanking gay quarters. Bibliography and index.

Lin Yü-t'ang, " *On Charm in Women,*" China Critic, 1936, vol. XII.
An article which includes a partial translation of Li Yü's 李漁 writings about perfection in women, with details about life in the women's quarters. (Cf. van Gulik, *op. cit.*, 302, comments about Li Yü's *Ou-chi* 偶集.)

Lü T'ien-ch'eng 呂天成. *Hsiu-t'a yeh-shih* 繡榻野史. Edition not located.
A late Ming novel about the sexual orgies of a heterosexual, his family members and his friends. (Described in van Gulik, *op. cit.*, 313–14.)

Martin, Richard, tr. (from the German translation of Franz Kuhn). Li Yü, *Jou Pu Tuan* (" The Prayer Mat of Flesh "). Grove Press, New York, 1963.
A readable account of the amorous adventures of a young and talented scholar. (Cf. van Gulik, *op. cit.*, 303–6, for a long translated extract from the novel.)

Miall, B., tr. from Franz Kuhn's abbreviated version of *Chin P'ing Mei*. New York, Capricorn, 1960.
Arthur Waley contributes an introduction to this abridgement, in which he discusses the problem of authorship. (Cf. Ming: Hanan, P. D.)

Miao Chüan-sun 繆荃孫. *Ch'in-huai kuang-chi* 奏淮廣記. Commercial Press, Shanghai, 1924 (photolithographed edition).
A voluminous record of facts about how prostitution flourished at Nanking from the start of Ming onwards. Many primary sources are cited.

Ono, Shinobu, " *Chin P'ing Mei: A Critical Study*," Acta Asiatica No. 5 (1963), The Tōhō Gakkai, Tokyo, 1963, 76–89.
A study of editions, not as " critical " or detailed as Hanan's articles, q.v.

Ono, Shinobu 小野忍 and Chida Kuichi 千田九一, tr. *Kin Pei Bai* 金瓶梅. Heibonsha, Tokyo, 1962, 3 vols.
Complete Japanese translation of *Chin P'ing Mei*, with detailed annotation at the end of each chapter and, following the translation, an essay on editions and a literary critique of the novel.

Otten, Otto and Arthur, tr. *Djin ping mei, Schlehen blüten in goldener Vase.* Facker verlag, 1965, illustrated.

P'an Chih-heng 潘之恆. *Chin-ling chi-p'in* 金陵妓品. In *Shuo-fu (hsü)*, vol. 44.
Four categories of feminine excellence, each followed by a brief listing of prostitute names.

P'an Chih-heng 潘之恒. *Ch'ü-li chih* 曲里志. (or *Ch'ü-chung chih* 曲中志). In *Shuo-fu (hsü)*, vol. 44.
A late Ming reminiscence of the gay quarters at Nanking, recording brief vignettes of superlative prostitutes.

P'an Chih-heng. *Ch'ü yen-p'in* 曲艷品. In *Shuo-fu (hsü)*, vol. 44.
The expounding of a thesis which likens musical instruments to feminine beauties.

Pan Tzu-yen. *The Reminiscences of Tung Hsiao-wan.* Commercial Press, Shanghai, 1961.
Translation and original text of the love reminiscences of Ming scholar Mao Hsiang (1611–1693) about a deceased concubine (see van Gulik, *op. cit.*, 291–4).

Schlegel, G. *Le Vendeur d'huile qui seul possède la Reine-de-Beauté, ou Splendeurs et Misères des Courtisanes chinoises.* Brill and Maisonneuve, Leyden and Paris, 1877.

A French translation of a Ming story which provides a description of brothel life. The original Chinese text is included. In his preface, the translator describes a visit that he and some friends made in 1861 to a " flower-boat " of prostitution at Canton.

Suzuki Shinkai 鈴木直海. *Enofu* 鴛鴦譜. Shina bunken kankōkai, Tokyo, 1915.

This work, which was not for sale, is representative of the many publications on Sino-Japanese sexological subjects which have been privately printed and distributed. It contains four translations of stories in the Ming collection, *Ku-chin ch'i-kuan* 古今奇観.

T'ang Yin 唐寅. *Seng-ni nieh-hai* 僧尼孽海. Undated manuscript copy, 2 vols.

There are twenty-six stories attributed to T'ang Yin in this collection entitled, " Monks and Nuns in a Sea of Sins." The stories are extremely erotic, with concentration on the sexual act and exaggerated narration of masculine prowess and feminine response. As van Gulik notes (*Sexual Life*, 320–1), it uses many sexual terms found in the old sex handbooks. Sexual terms of much later date are also plentiful.

Teng Hsi-hsien 登希賢. *Tz'u-chin kuang-yüeh ta-hsien hsiu-chen yen-i* 紫金光耀大仙修眞演義. Ming blockprint, 1598, other editions as well (see van Gulik, *op. cit.*, 280–5).

A text on the pros and cons of sexual intercourse, which includes a list of sexual aids and other items of special interest not found elsewhere.

Ts'ao Ta-chang 曹大章. *Ch'in-huai shih-nü piao* 秦淮士女表. In *Shuo-fu* (*hsü*), vol. 44.

A late Ming reminiscence of the gay quarters at Nanking, in which superlative beauties are likened to academic categories. The brief ranking of beauties is preceded by a long introductory essay.

Ts'ao Ta-chang. *Kuang-ling nü-shih tien-tsui* 廣陵女士殿最. In *Shuo-fu* (*hsü*), vol. 44.

An essay which exclaims on feminine and flowery charms, emphasizing the feminine qualities of certain flowers.

Ts'ao Ta-chang. *Lien-t'ai hsien-hui p'in* 蓮臺仙會品. In *Shuo-fu* (*hsü*), vol. 44.

A brief essay on how the writer and his fellow voluptuaries considered gradations of beauty.

Ts'ao Ta-chang 曹大章. *Yen-tu chi-p'in* 燕都妓品. In *Shuo-fu (hsü)*, vol. 44.
A late Ming account of brothel life in Peking, with varied references to beauty and beauties. It includes many quotes from T'ang poets.

Tu Tse 杜澤, compiler. *Hung-wu ching-ch'eng t'u-chih* 洪武京城圖志. Wood-block edition, preface dated 1395.
One map in this collection shows the location of prostitution houses in Nanking; there is also a list of sites in the prostitution compound.

van Gulik, R. H. *Erotic colour prints of the Ming period, with an essay on Chinese sex life from the Han to the Ch'ing dynasty, B. C. 206–A. D. 1644;* privately printed, edition limited to 50 copies for presentation to libraries and research centers; 1957.
The analysis of Chinese sex life in its social context which preceded Dr. van Gulik's monograph on the subject. (see *General: Sexual Life in Ancient China.*) Dr. van Gulik, who reproduced prints from one Ming album of visual erotica, included in this monograph many translations from ancient Taoist texts. In the second section, there is a detailed description of late Ming erotica albums, materials dealt with more fully in *Sexual Life . . .,* 322–33. See both works for all citations to such albums.

van Gulik, R. H. *Trifling Tale of a Spring Dream* (春夢瑣言), privately printed in 200 copies, Tokyo, 1950, 6 page introduction followed by 19 pages of Chinese text.
The reprint of a Ming erotic text published from a reprint preserved in Japan. If authentic in date, this text shows that *Yu-hsien k'u* was known in China in the seventeenth century, for the plot is very similar. There is, however, much more description of sex-play in this text than in the T'ang novelette.

Wrenn, James Joseph. *Texual Method and its Application to Texts of the Chin P'ing Mei.* Yale University, 1964, thesis.

IX. CH'ING

Arène, Jules. *La Chine familière.* Charpentier, Paris, 1883 (2nd edition).
An account based on twelve years of residence which stresses exotic aspects of Chinese songs, plays, and customs. Some information on Cantonese boat prostitution, in semi-fictional form.

Chao Chih-hsin 趙執信. *Hai-ou hsiao-p'u* 海鷗小譜. In Chao-tai ts'ung-shu pieh-chi 昭代叢書別集.
Poetic essays in a " woman-flower " vein, with ten curtailed verse about unforgettable beauties.

Hsi-hsi shan-jen 西溪山人 (pseudonym; 19th century). *Wu-men hua-fang lu* 吳門畫舫錄. In Shuang-mei ching-an ts'ung-shu.
Essay on prostitution around Hangchow in the nineteenth century (see Ch'ing: Iwaki).

Iwaki Hideo 岩城秀夫. *Hankyō zakki. Soshū gahōroku* 板橋雜記・蘇州画舫錄, Heibonsha, Tokyo, 1964.
Annotated translations of a late Ming text on the prostitution quarters at Nanking (see Levy, H. S., tr., Yü Huai) and a Ch'ing essay on the floating brothels at Suchou in the nineteenth century. The introductions, translations, and notes are carefully done.

Jametel, Maurice. *La Chine Inconnue.* Paris, 1884.
I have not seen this work, but Robert Des Rotours states that, on pp. 215–46, it provides a description of boatside prostitution as it existed in Canton in about 1880. (See Des Rotours, *Courtisanes Chinoises a la fin des T'ang*, 31.)

Joly, H. Bencraft. *Hung Lou Meng; or The Dream of the Red Chamber.* Kelly and Walsh, Hong Kong, 1892; 2 vols.
A full but incomplete translation of this Chinese love classic.

Kean, Vladimir, abridged trans. of Franz Kuhn's trans. of *Ko-lien hua-ying* 隔簾花影 ("*Flower Shadows Behind the Curtain*"), The Bodley Head, London, 1959.
A sequel to *Chin P'ing Mei*, written in the Ch'ing dynasty, centering around most of the original characters of the Ming novel. Ch'ing authorities forbade its circulation. (see Wylie, *Notes on Chinese Literature*, XXII.)

Kuhn, Franz, tr. *Der Traum der Roten Kammer.* Insel Verlag, Leipzig, undated.
The least abridged translation of *Hung-lou meng.* (see Wang; Joly)

Levy, Howard S., "*Introduction to 'A Celestial Bedside Manual'*", Orient/West, vol. 8, no. 4, July-August, 1963, 100–2.
Describes two essays of early and late Ch'ing times for and against polygamy, written in a light and witty vein. (See Idem., *Warm-Soft Village*.)

Lin Yü-t'ang. *The Importance of Living* (New York, 1938); see ch. 10 for a partial translation of Chiang T'an's 蔣坦 *Ch'iu-teng so-i* 秋燈瑣憶.
A scholar's reminiscence of a favored concubine.

Lin Yü-t'ang. *Six Chapters of a Floating Life;* tr. of Shen Fu's 沈復 *Fou-sheng liu-chi* 浮生六記. T'ien-hsia Monthly, Hong Kong, 1935, vol. 1.
Autobiographical account of a Ch'ing painter-poet, describing his wife, who died soon after their marriage.

Matignon, Dr. J. J. *La Chine Hermétique.* Paris, 1936.
Reprint of a 1902 edition, in which a French doctor in Peking at the turn of the century discoursed on footbinding, homosexuality and other practices, in a somewhat sinophobic vein.

Schlegel, Gustav. *Histoire de la Prostitution en Chine.* Rouen, 1880.
Despite its title, this monograph deals mainly with prostitution in south China in the late nineteenth century, based on the author's observations.

Schlegel, G., " *Iets over de Prostitutie in China,*" Verhandelungen van Bataviaasch genotschab 32 (1866). Also a separate publication—Lange, Batavia (Netherlands East Indies), 1866.

Shutze, Adolph, tr. *China und die Chinesen,* von Tscheng Ki-tong, 2 Auflage, Reissner, Dresden, 1896.

St. Julien. *Les Deux Cousines.* Paris, 1864. Translation of a Ch'ing novel about love, called *Yü-chiao-li* 王嬌梨.
A minor novel about love among literati, with a few homosexual implications (see can Gulik, *op. cit.,* 296 n).

Tcheng Ki-tong, " La Chine et les Chinois " (an article in three parts), Revue des Deux Mondes, IIIe Pér., 63 (1884. 3), 278–305, 596–622, 820–55.
A general introduction to life and customs, including specific sections on " La Femme " and " Les Plaisirs."

Wang Chi-chen, tr. *The Dream of the Red Chamber (Hung-lou meng).* London and New York, 1929.
An abridged translation of China's most famous love classic, portraying feelings of delicacy and refinement.

Wylie, A. *Notes on Chinese Literature.* Paragon reprint, New York, 1964.
This work by Wylie, compiled in 1867, contains a list of 137 works that the Ching authorities ordered kept out of circulation because, in Wylie's words, they were of a "treasonable or licentious tendency." (Introduction, XXII–XXIII.)

Yang En-shou 揚恩壽. *Lan-chih ling-hsiang lu* 蘭芷零香録. In T'an-yüan ch'üan-chi 坦園全集.
Biographies of famous beauties, followed by anecdotes about wine and the pleasure quarters, with relevant selections from poetry and prose.

Yen-pei lao-jen 燕北老人 (pseudonym). *Man-ch'ing shih-san ch'ao kung-wei mi-shih* 滿清十三朝宮闈秘史. Ta Chung-ku t'u-shu yu-hsien kung-ssu, Taipei, 1956.
Fictionalized elaboration of harem incidents; supported by considerable historical investigation. Presented in general chronological order, and

followed by about fifty pages on harem conditions during *T'ai-p'ing* rule.

Yü Chiao 俞蛟. *Ch'ao-chia feng-yüeh chi* 潮嘉風月記. In Chao-tai ts'ung-shu pieh-chi 昭代叢書別集.
A miscellaneous record of facts on such subjects as women, musical instruments, opium, tea, and local customs, with an emphasis on prostitution and the prostitution quarters.

X. REPUBLIC

Chang Ching-sheng 張競生. *Ai-ch'ing ting-tse t'ao-lun chi* 愛情定則討論集.
Good Youth Library, Shanghai, 1929, 272 pages; rare copy in the Columbia University library.
Research attributed to the famed sexologist Chang Ching-sheng, in conjunction with a " Miss B ", on the principles of love. It includes letters and answers by Dr. Chang to questions of his correspondents. He also discourses in general terms on the nature of love, placing his comments within a Chinese social context. Other viewpoints are also represented. Some of these materials were first published in 1923, in the Peking Press.

Ch'i-ch'i nü-shih 綺綺女士 (pseudonym). *Shao-nien nan-nü hsing wen-ta* 少年男女性問答. Chien-k'ang ch'u-pan she 健康出版社, undated (1967?).
Advice on a wide range of questions submitted by Chinese youths, providing guidance on sexual conduct before and after marriage. References are occasionally made to traditional Chinese sex practices. The general tenor is conservative. Masturbation and nocturnal emissions are frowned upon, with exercise and athletic activities recommended as remedies. This Hong Kong publisher specializes in small modern sex-guidance publications, listing a dozen titles in a back-cover advertisement.

Chin Jung 金榮. *Hsing sheng-huo yen-chiu* 性生活研究. Hsin-hsin shu-chü 新新書局, Taiwan, 1962.
Detailed explanation of sexual procedures, with emphasis on biological knowledge and psychological preparedness. A generally Western-oriented approach.

K'ang Erh-lang 康爾朗 and others, tr. Masters-Johnson study, *Human Sexual Response*, Kuo-ts'ui shu-pao she 國粹書報社, Taipei, 1966.
This complete translation was compiled by a team of four translators; three specialists in medical aspects, and one collator. The sale of a work like this in translation indicates that Western sexological information is now made quickly available to Chinese in Taiwan. (Chinese sexological publications in Hong Kong are also up-to-date.)

Levy, Howard S., tr. Chang Ching-sheng 張競生. *Hsing-shih* 性史 ("*Sex Histories: China's First Modern Treatise on Sex Education* "), Haku-ensha, Yokohama, 1968 (mimeographed).

A translation from the Japanese text of the accounts of early sex experiences by six young Chinese men and women, in the nineteen twenties, analyzed as to sexological import by Dr. Chang Ching-sheng.

Nakayama Motosuke 中山素輔, tr. Chang Ching-sheng 張競生. *Chūgoku seishi. Sojokyō* 中國性史・素女經, Tokyo, Murasaki shobō 紫書房, September 5, 1951.

Translation into Japanese of Chang Ching-sheng's compilation of sex histories (see Republic: Levy, *Sex Histories*) and Yeh Teh-hui's editorial rearrangement according to sex handbooks of parts of the twenty-eighth section of *The Essence of Medical Prescriptions* 医心方. (See T'ang: Yeh Teh-hui, *So-nü ching*.)

T'ao Han-ts'ui 陶寒翠. *Min-kuo yen-shih yen-i* 民國艶史演義. Shanghai, Shih-huan shu-chü 時還書局, 1929 (?), 8 vols. of 120 sex adventures, 1 vol. of illustrations.

These stories are about the amorous activities of warlords and bureaucrats active in China from 1911 to 1928; they are all written in modern collo-quial style. The non-erotic illustrations depict incidents referred to in the stories.

Yao Ling-hsi 兆靈犀. *P'ing-wai wei-yen* 瓶外危信. Saika shorin 採華書林, known prior to April, 1961 as Tenzan shoten 天山書店, Tokyo, 1961. A reprint of the 1940 Chinese edition.

Yao Ling-hsi describes more than a thousand expressions of sexual import not found in *Chin P'ing Mei*. (For bibliographical descriptions of Yao Ling-hsi's monographs on footbinding, see Five Dynasties and Sung; Levy, *Chinese Footbinding: The Story of a Curious Erotic Custom*.)

B. Japan

I. GENERAL

See China, General: Report to the Council.

* Hayashi Wakaki 林若樹, ed. *Uma no haru* 午の春 (" Spring in the Year of the Horse "), Tokyo, privately printed catalogue, 1930.

This catalogue of old Japanese sex books was compiled by Hayashi Wakaki, a rich man from Kobe. It consisted of about 30 books in his personal collection, which were all sold after his death. The catalogue is introduced with a poem about the editor's showing the sex books to his friends in the spring of the year of the horse (1930), with the implication that, since the horse is known for its large penis, it was appropriate to publish the catalogue in that year.

Hisamatsu Sen'ichi, " *The Characteristics of Beauty in the Japanese Middle Ages,*" Acta Asiatica, No. 8, 1965, 40–53.

* Ikeda Yasaburō 池田弥三郎 and others. *Sei fūzoku* 性風俗, *Dai san-shū* 第三集, Yūsan-kaku 雄山閣, Tokyo, 1959, profusely illustrated; bibliography and index.

Seven Japanese university professors collaborated in compiling this volume on sexual customs. The work contains a wealth of little-known information, and is thoroughly indexed for easy reference. The numerous illustrations enhance textual comments.

* Mayabara Nario 馬屋原成男, editor. *Kaishaku to kanshō* 解釈と鑑賞, Shibundō, Tokyo.

Originated in 1932, this is an excellent journal devoted to the scholarly analysis of Japanese literary works. In its last three special issues devoted to erotica, its contributors have listed hundreds of items openly or privately published, either little known or unknown in the West. A fourth issue on erotica is scheduled for publication in 1969.

Abbreviation: KK

Miyatake Gaikotsu 宮武外骨. *Jakumetsu iraku kō* 寂滅為楽考. Tokyo, undated (ca. 1930 ?).

A brief treatise cited by van Gulik, *op. cit.*, 304n, about the exclamations of women when they have orgasms. Mr. Miyatake was a great collector of erotica, but on his death the collection he had assembled over the years was dispersed. (Information supplied by Dr. Ishihara in the summer of 1968.)

Sakai Kiyoshi 酒井潔. *Ai no majutsu* 愛の魔術. Kokusai bunken kankōkai, Tokyo, 1929.
A rambling description of magic potions and formulae used to enhance love. The writer includes an explanation of the love meaning of hexagrams in the *Book of Changes* and refers frequently to Western phenomena.

II. HEIAN

Iida Yoshirō 飯田吉郎, "*Dōgenshi*" 洞玄子, KK, 7/68, 211–219.
Professor Iida translated into Japanese the writings of Tung Hsüan-tzu as found in the 28th section of *Ishimpō* 医心方, affixing Japanese readings to the characters. A few explanatory notes are appended to the translation.

Iida Yoshirō 飯田吉郎, "*Ishimpō bōnaihen sho*" 医心方房内篇書, KK, 4/67, 20–33.
Professor Iida has translated into Japanese the 4th to 12th, 14th, 15th and 18th chapters of the twenty-eighth section of *Ishimpō*, reproducing at the top of each page the original texts from which the translations were made.

Sugi Yasusaburō 杉靖三郎, "*Ishimpō bōnaihen*" 医心方房内篇, KK, 4/67, 9–19.
A general introduction to *Ishimpō*, with a listing of 80 Sui-T'ang works cited in it. The writer then describes the 28th section and gives a general analysis of its contents, with appropriate citations. Professor Sugi also shows the ways in which passages from *Ishimpō* were incorporated into Yōjōkun (see Yedo: Kaibara).

Takikawa Masajirō 滝川政次郎, "*Heian jidai no himerareta bungaku*" 平安時代の秘められた文学, KK, 10/64, 18–24.
A well-organized and scholarly article which discusses several short erotic literary works of the Heian era in which the writer's true name was concealed. Difficult sexual terms are clearly and adequately explained. The writer presents a poem about the delights of sexual intercourse attributed to Po Hsing-chien 白行簡, the younger brother of Po Chü-i, and while not translating it provides some annotation. The origins of erotic Chinese literature are attributed to the end of the Six Dynasties period which preceded the T'ang. Japanese living in Sui China, concludes the writer, were the first to bring boudoir compositions to Japan.

Tanaka Ichimatsu 田中一松 and Miya Tsugio 宮次男, "*Kodai, chūsei no higakan*" 古代, 中世の秘画巻, KK, 10/64. 244–50.
An article which traces the history of visual eroticism from the ninth to fourteenth centuries, based on literary and historical evidence. The

writers stress the fact that several collections featured illustrations of homosexual love, a theme especially popular during the Kamakura era.

* Yoshida Takashi 吉田隆, and others. *Ishimpō bōnai* 医心方房内. Haga shoten 芳賀書店, Tokyo, August, 1968; illustrated.
When this study came to our attention our monograph, except for the bibliography and index, was already being processed at the printer's. It consists of a few erotic illustrations, a chapter on the medical and sexual significance of the text, a diagram showing the external female sex organs, a list of important works cited in the 28th chapter of *Ishimpō*, and a Japanese translation (without the Chinese text) which is more colloquial and less literal than that done by Dr. Ishihara in 1967. It uses black figures, rather inelegantly drawn, for the illustrations of sex positions. Photographs of medicines mentioned in the text and annotations concerning them have been placed in the last section (240–302). On certain half-pages, there are translated extracts from a treatise called *Lin-lang fou-chi* 琳琅浮記, on types of feminine sexual organs and special terminology (cited as being in a Peking work called *Hsing-shih* 性史, collection 10, Peking, *Wen-hua shu-she* 文化書社, n.d.).

III. KAMAKURA-MUROMACHI

See Heian: Tanaka

Fujioka Sakutarō 藤岡作太郎. *Kamakura Muromachi jidai bungakushi* 鎌倉室町時代文學史, Iwanami shoten, Tokyo, 1949.
Includes a chapter on love stories of the Muromachi era (301–07), stating they were depicted in Heian-style. Eight stories are described, q.v.

Ishihara Akira 石原明, " *Tonishō* " 頓医抄, KK, 7/68, 9–26.
Dr. Ishihara provides bibiographical details on a Japanese medical work of the Kamakura era (completed in 1304) and reproduces its forty-fifth chapter, dealing with the bedroom arts and the efficaciousness of aphrodisiacs.

Nakagawa Zenkyō 中川善教, "*Tachikawa-ryū*" 立川流, KK, 7/68, 235–46.
The writer explains the doctrines of a heterodox and outlawed 12th-century sect which stressed the inextricable relationship of sexual knowledge and religious development.

Tamba Yukinaga 丹波行長. *Eisei hiyōshō* 衛生秘要抄. In Zoku gunsho ruijū 續群書類從, ch. 900 (Tokyo, 1931).
A Japanese text which Franke, DZMG, 1955, 387, cites as an example of how erotic terminology in the ancient Chinese handbooks of sex was inter-

preted by Japanese heirs to the *Ishimpō* tradition.

IV. MOMOYAMA

See China (Ming: Dr. Keizo Dohi)

Hamada Giichirō 浜田義一郎, " *Inu tsukubashū* " 犬つくば集, KK, 10/64, 36/46.
An article on humorous-erotic poems in linked style, on which two poets collaborated. The first gave the final three lines (5, 7, 7 syllables), the second added the initial lines (5, 7 syllables). One of these representative " poetic-challenge " poems alluded to a woman's sexual organs.

Kaneko Matabē 金子又兵衛, " *Kyōunshū* " 狂雲集, KK, 10/64, 29–35.
Comments about poems written by a Zen Buddhist priest which blended religious concepts with sex. The poems were assembled by disciples in various editions, which the writer discusses.

Ozaki Hisaya 尾崎久弥, " *Kōshoku ume no hanagaki* " 好色梅の花垣, KK, 4/67, 34–46.
Detailed analysis of the extant second volume of an erotically illustrated storybook, which the investigator surmises to date from about the middle of the sixteenth century.

V. YEDO

Asano Kenji 浅野建二, " *Yedo jidai no zokuyō* " 江戸時代の俗謡, KK, 10/64, 161–72.
Clearly traces popular songs in several Yedo collections with hidden or overt sexual meanings, fully explaining metaphors and references.

Fushimi Chūkei 伏見冲敬, " *Daitō keigo* " 大東閨語, KK, 10/64, 83–96.
Scholarly study of a late Yedo work on relations between the sexes, in the form of 33 stories about famous men and beautiful women that range in time from the Nara to Kamakura eras.

Fushimi Chūkei 伏見冲敬, " *Shunran sekkō* 春蘭折甲, KK, 4/67, 81–94.
Describes a 30 page work written in *kambun* in about 1763, which revealed influences from Chinese erotic literature. The story, illustrated, is about the love emotions of a young bureaucrat.

Hamada Giichirō 浜田義一郎, " *Shunsō hiji* " 春窓秘辞, KK, 4/67, 101–13.
A study of the compositions which twelve famous early nineteenth century

writers affixed in a spirit of amusement to calendar illustrations of women.

Hamada Kenji, tr. Saikaku's *The Life of an Amorous Man*. Tuttle, Vermont, 1964; illustrated.

Hasegawa Tsuyoshi 長谷川強, "*Yahaku naishō kagami*" 野白内證鑑, KK, 4/67, 47–61.

Describes a sex manual in the form of a dialogue between a man and a woman, the Preface of which is dated 1710.

Hasegawa Tsuyoshi 長谷川強, "*Zunanbutsu*" 豆男物, KK, 10/64, 57–66.
A wide-ranging discussion of erotic Yedo literature, with references to many different works.

* Hayashi Yoshikazu 林美一, "*Shimpen kōshokuhon shunga mokuroku*" 新編好色本春画目録, KK, 7/68, 160–210.
This is an extremely important article. Professor Hayashi, who is assembling a bibliography of erotic literature of the Yedo period, has already uncovered close to 3,000 items. In this article he describes the characteristics of erotic writings of the Yedo era and mentions his earlier articles on erotic Yedo works printed in twelve issues of *Kinsei shomin bunka* 近世庶民文化 (not publicly available). He further cites earlier bibliographical studies on Yedo erotica that he consulted, and then lists more than 400 works arranged according to the Japanese syllabary, from あ to こ.

Hayashi Yoshikazu 林美一, "*Shunjō gidan mizuage chō*" 春情妓談水揚帖, KK, 7/68, 115–45.
A famed book of late Yedo era illustrations depicting sexual life. It was one of five major works by the artist Ryūtei Tanehiko 柳亭種彦, and appeared in 1836. The title refers to a geisha's deflowering by the highest bidder.

Hibbett, Howard. *The Floating World in Japanese Fiction*. Oxford University Press, London, 1959, illustrated.
An entertaining and readable account of Japanese fiction of the late 17th and early 18th centuries, with translated extracts from Saikaku's *The Woman Who Spent Her Life in Love*.

Hirota Masanjin 広田魔山人, "*Kagetsu chō*" 華月帖, KK, 4/67, 74–80.
Analysis of an erotic album published in 1836, with an explanation of the Preface, content of the illustrations, and the attendant calligraphy. Includes a biography of the album's compiler, Kamo Suetaka 加茂季鷹.

Hirota Masanjin 広田魔山人, "*Shumpūchō*" 春風帖, KK, 7/68, 100–9.
The original author, Nakajima Sōin 中島棕隠, printed one volume in 1856 and intended to print a second volume but was unable to complete the project. Mr. Nakajima was a Confucian scholar who used Ming-Ch'ing

literary styles to write twelve Japanese erotic stories, which are very difficult to understand. The work was printed one year after the author's death.

Jimbo Itsuya 神保五弥, " *Hatsuhana* " はつはな, KK, 7/68, 110–14.
The author is not known, but the writer deduces from the calligraphic evidence that he was the famous 19th-century literatus Yashiro Hirokata 屋代弘賢. The illustrator was the equally famous Kita Takekiyo 喜多武清. The story, a fictional account of the love between a Minamoto hero and a Taira heroine, is written in difficult Heian style.

* Jimbo Itsuya 神保五弥, " *Yedo kinsho kaidai* " 江戸禁書解題, KK, 10/64, 202–18.
A history of the official steps taken by the Shogunate to prohibit publication and sale of erotic and other works considered injurious to the preservation of social customs. There are many references to prohibited books.

Kaibara Ekken 貝原益軒. *Yōjōkun*. *Wazoku dōshikun* 養生訓. 和俗童子訓, Iwanami, Tokyo, 1967 (4th edition).
This is a reprint in reduced size of two early 18th-century works, the first dealing with the cultivation of life and the second with education from childhood onwards. In *Yōjōkun* (pp. 96–100), ancient Taoist sexology works and the Confucian Analects are cited to support the view that sexual restraint is a prerequisite to health and longevity.

Kodaka Toshirō 小高敏郎, " *Sakujitsu wa konnichi no monogatari* " 昨日は今日の物語, KK, 10/64, 47–66.
Scholarly discussion of an early Yedo fictional work which alluded to the profligate behavior of youths and monks.

Mayabara Nario 馬屋原成男, " *Nagamakura shitone gassen* " to " *Hana no miyuki* " 長枕褥合戦と花の幸, KK, 4/67, 62–73.
Professor Mayabara describes two 18th-century love stories which focused on the largeness of the hero's penis.

Miyao Shigeo 宮尾しげを, " *Enshoku kobanashi hon* " 艶色小噺本, KK, 10/64, 144–60.
An article about jokebooks of the Yedo era, mostly concerning sexual puns, with selected extracts.

Morris, Ivan, tr. and ed. Ihara Saikaku's *The Life of an Amorous Woman and Other Writings*, New Directions, Norfolk, 1963.
Annotated translation about a nymphomaniac in the gay quarters, with emphasis on her physical decline and social descent. The translator discusses the whole range of Saikaku's fiction, erotic and otherwise (23–39),

and includes a section on sources (267–81).

* Muto Sadao 武藤禎夫, " *Yedo enshō kobanashi shugyokushū* " 江戸艶笑小咄珠玉集, KK, 4/67, 163–85.
A valuable article on erotic humor which has many bibliographical references to similar studies. It also records stories from about 20 different works, divided by subject.

Nakano Mitsutoshi 中野三敏, " *Hihon shūi* " 秘本拾遺, KK, 10/64, 67–82.
Describes several literary works privately printed during the early 18th century, when publications of erotic content were officially prohibited.

* Nishimura Sadamasa 西村定雅 (as ascertained by Takahashi Tetsu). *Shikidō kimpishō* 色道禁秘抄, Amatoriasha あまとりあ社, Tokyo, 1962 (5th printing), arranged in folio form.
This is a reprint of a Japanese classic compiled in 1834, called *A Summation of the Forbidden Secrets of the Way of Sex*. Takahashi Tetsu 高橋鐵 has appended a detailed and valuable commentary to all sections of the original work. Its sixty-four brief chapters contain question-answer dialogues reminiscent of the Chinese sex handbook, dealing with varied aspects of man-woman boudoir relations and generally advocating continence and self-control.

Oba Shunsuke 大場俊助, " *Issa seikō no kiroku* " 一茶性交の記録, KK, 7/68, 114–62.
Detailed commentary on and extensive abstracts from the diary of the Haiku poet Issa, specifically the portions in which he reveals aspects of his sex life. Clear and masterly organization and presentation of the materials.

Okada Hajime 岡田甫, " *Anaokashi* " 阿奈遠加志, KK, 4/67, 200–19.
A study of the second of three so-called " curious works " 奇書 of the period. It is shown to contain much erotic humor and wit, couched in elegant style. There is considerable information on author, editions, and time of compilation, after which selections from its stories are presented and translated into modern colloquial Japanese. Very good scholarly investigation.

Okada Hajime 岡田甫, " *Hakoya no Himegoto* " はこやのひめごと, KK, 10/64, 111–34.
This is the first of three studies, each devoted to an analysis of the so-called three " curious works " 奇書 of the Yedo period. (Cf. KK, 4/67, 200–219; 7/68, 73–99.) In this article, Professor Okada introduces all three works and describes one in depth (藐姑射秘言), with detailed annotation.

Okada Hajime 岡田甫, " *Itsuchomonshū* " 逸著聞集, KK, 7/68, 73–99.
Professor Okada describes the third of three so-called " curious works "
of the Yedo period. The third work is a collection of 58 stories, more than
half of which are drawn from earlier literary sources. They stress erotic
humor. About ten of the *Itsuchomonshū* stories are recorded, annotated,
and fully explained.

Ōmura Shage 大村沙華, " *Shunjō harusame goromo* " 春情春雨衣, KK, 7/68,
146–59.
The author was Baitei Kinga 梅亭金鵞 (1821–1893), the illustrator Ume-
no-moto Osai 梅の本鶯斎, and their book was printed in 1858. It con-
cerns a love story at Atami and the elopment of the lovers. The man consequently lives happily together with this mistress, whom he wives, and his
first wife and child.

Ōmura Shage 大村沙華, " *Yanagi no hazue* " 柳の葉末, KK, 4/67, 186–99.
Professor Ōmura describes a pornographic book published in 1835 which
was prohibited from sale till the post-war period. He gives details about
author and publication, and supplies extracts and learned analyses of a
work he calls " evil " and of little literary worth.

Ozaki Hisaya 尾崎久弥, " *Kōshoku tamagozake* " 好色玉子酒, KK, 7/68,
52–72.
First publication of the text of an illustrated story of love adventures from
the Genroku era, which appeared at the start of the 18th century. Two
of the five chapters are no longer extant. The text preserves colloquial
usage of the times.

Taikyokudō Arinaga 大極堂有長 (pseudonym). *Shikidō kimpishō* 色道禁秘抄.
Tokyo, Hsinryūsha, 1964.
Reprint of the original sexological treatise of 1834, without comment.
This work also contains Japanese translations of *Ch'ing-shih* 情史 and
So-nü-ching 素女經, apparently copied in their entirety from the translation
published in 1951 by Nakayama Motosuke. (See *China : Republic* ; Naka-
yama Motosuke.)

Takehara Shōkaku 竹原松鶴, " *Kōshoku kunmō zui* " 好色訓蒙図彙, KK,
7/68, 37–51.
An illustrated work of the Genroku era which, using fictional materials
of the times, has been called an encyclopedia of sex and love. Its contents are described and quoted, and its value as a repository of customs
and aspects of its times is shown.

Tanabe Teinosuke 田辺貞之助. *Kobanashi Suetsumuhana shō* こばなし末

摘花抄; *Extrait de Suetsumuhana-annote humoristequement.* Kōbunsha 高文社, Tokyo, 1961.
Professor Tanabe of Tokyo University furnishes non-technical explanations of several hundred erotic *senryū* in *Suetsumuhana*, arranged by subject categories. He relates relevant stories of the Yedo era and introduces French stories written in a similar vein. A unique study.

Usuda Jingorō 臼田甚五郎, " *Yedo jidai no shunka* " 江戸時代の春歌, KK, 4/67, 220–45.
A study of the texts of Yedo love-songs; Mr. Usuda refers to an earlier article of his in KK, 6/66, describing a peasant festival in Akita and Yamagata in which naked husband and wife prayed for agrarian abundance while looking at each other's sex organs.

Yoshida Seiichi 吉田精一, " *Shidōken gohekiron* " 志道軒五癖論, KK, 4/67, 95–100.
The story of a mid-18th-century personality called Shidōken, who would lecture on erotic subjects to groups who recompensed him with contributions of money. He lectured at the Kannon Temple garden in Asakusa, holding up a wooden model of a penis and explaining five types of feminine sexual reactions. His writings about this were later transformed into literary style, and the resultant essay was printed in June 1952 in the twelfth issue of the journal *Kinsei shomin bunka* 近世庶民文化 (not publicly available).

VI MEIJI

Anonymous. *Notes on the History of the Yoshiwara of Yedo.* Printed at the " Japan Gazette " office, 1894.
A brief but information-filled pamphlet (22 pages) setting forth a history of the Yoshiwara, with diagrams of the new and old quarter and of third and fourth class brothels.

Aston, W. G. *A History of Japanese Literature.* D. Appleton, New York, 1914.
Describes the *Ninjōbon*, late 19th-century fictional works about common feelings (376–79), and the best known writer in this genre, Tamenaga Shunsui, who died in 1842 while confined to his house in handcuffs—for publishing books prejudicial to public morals.

* De Becker, J. E. *The Nightless City.* Box of Curios Printing Company, Yokohama, 1905 (third edition), illustrated.

This is a superb study of the Yoshiwara, the leading quarter of prostitution in Tokyo, while it was flourishing. The author provides a detailed history of the Yoshiwara and translates many documents pertaining to general regulations, medical inspections, and brothel control. We lack such information for the famed Chinese prostitution quarters of the past.

* Jō Ichirō 城市郎. *Zoku hakkimbon* 続発禁本. Tōgensha 桃源社, Tokyo, 1965 ; 62 illustrations.
A valuable monograph in which the author analyzes in detail Meiji and post-Meiji Japanese works that have been officially prohibited from sale and concludes with a chapter on Western erotica in Japanese translation. He cites his earlier monograph, *Hakkimbon* 発禁本 (図書新聞連載). Consult this work for many items of erotica not cited in our bibliography.

* Mayabara Nario 馬屋原成男, " *Meiji, Taisho, Shōwa hakkinsho kaidai* " 明治, 大正, 昭和發禁書解題, KK, 10/64, 219–43.
An article on book-banning which has detailed comments on censorship and regulation during the Meiji era. Book and article references are precise, with publishers cited. The article concludes with a brief description of the early post-war period.

Ogawa Kazuzane 小川一眞. *Yoshiwara, A Nightless Quarter*. Ogawa shashin seihansho 小川寫眞製版所, Tokyo, 1910.
A photograph book of the Yoshiwara, printed on linen and in color. One photo shows prostitutes on exhibition. The writer stresses the superiority of the licensed Yoshiwara quarter to random streetwalking.

Soeda Tomomichi 添田知道, " *Meiji, Taishō jidai no shunka* " 明治, 大正時代の春歌, KK, 4/67, 246–62.
This article on pornographic illustrations describes the contents of two volumes which became well known at the start of the Meiji era, recording the calligraphy and providing readings for rarely-encountered compounds listed in these volumes.

Tresmin-Tremolieres. *Yoshiwara Die Liebesstadt der Japaner*. Louis Marcus Verlagsbuchhandlung, Sexualpsychologische Bibliothek, Berlin, 1899.
A thorough account of the history and the class and economic structures of the Yoshiwara bordellos. There is a Russian translation of this work ; *Gorod Liuvi* (" City of Love "). N. M. Lagova, St. Petersburg, 1905.

Yoshida Seiichi 吉田精一, " *Kyōshi* " 狂詩, KK, 10/64, 135–43.
An analysis of a few Chinese-style comic poems of the early Meiji era, in which drinking, wenching, and other social amusements are described. Various collections of these poems are cited.

VII. POST-MEIJI

See Meiji: Jō Ichirō.

See Meiji: Mayabara Nario, " *Meiji Taishō, Shōwa hakkinsho kaidai.*"

Balbi, B., tr. of Myu's *Le memorie di una geisha " Fuku-ko "*. L'Esteremo Urienta, Brescia, 1918.
Italian translation from the Japanese of a love reminiscence about a geisha called Fukuko.

De Bary, William T. *Five Women Who Loved Love*. Tuttle, Tokyo and Vermont, 1955.

* Editors, "*Atarashii fūfu seikatsu yōjōkun* " 新しい夫婦生活養生訓, Shūkan bunshun 週刊文春, Tokyo, April 15, 1968, 132–36.
A very interesting and instructive article in which modern views on sex of Japanese physicians are correlated with the sex advice in the early 18th century work *Yōjōkun* (see Yedo: Kaibara). A Japanese report on the frequency of intercourse is correlated with the Kinsey report (page 134), and reference is made to the technique of non-emission by the male as expounded in *Ishimpō*.

Fujimoto, T. *The Geisha Girl*. T. Werner Laurie, London, undated (1920–21 ?); profusely illustrated.
An insider's account of geisha life, with many individual sketches. An effort is made to understand the outlook of the geisha, who is regarded with sympathy and compassion.

Fujimoto, T. *The Nightside of Japan*, T. Werner Laurie, London, undated (about 1920 ?).
Detailed descriptions of nocturnal amusements in Tokyo, with a good sociological analysis of the prostitute quarters at Yoshiwara.

Gluck, Jay, ed. *Ukiyo: Stories of " The Floating World " of Postwar Japan*. Vanguard Press, New York, 1965.

* Kasano Umatarō 笠野馬太郎, " *Sengo hakkin shuppanbutsu mokuroku* " 戦後発禁出版物目録 (1947–1954), KK, 4/67, 263–83.
A very valuable article on published works whose sale was prohibited. Public and private works are listed by chronological order, with information provided when available on date and place of publication. The hundreds of listings include Western erotica as well.

Matsudo Hisashi 松戸尚. *Renzoku shashin de miru sei seikatsu* 連続写真で見る性生活. Yūki shobō 有紀書房, Tokyo, July, 1968; illustrated.

Woman shown alone, in different positions. A wide variety of diagrams, including those showing the sex organs during coitus. Detailed explanations.

Matsudo Hisashi 松戸尚. *Sei no nayami o kaiketsu suru hon* 性の悩みを解決する本. Yūki shobō, Tokyo, 1968(?) ; illustrated.
An illustrated work, one of a series, intended to solve the sexual problems of men and women from adolescence to old age. Pictures explained in simple colloquial Japanese.

Matsudo Hisashi. *Sei seikatsu kaibō zufu* 性生活解剖図譜. Yūki shobō, Tokyo, 1968(?), reprint ; illustrated.
A third work on positions in intercourse, matching pictures and text, with full-page illustrations.

Matsukubo Kōhei 松窪耕平. *Shashin to e de miru sei seikatsu* 写真と絵で見る性生活. Yūki shobō, Tokyo, June, 1967 (41st printing).
Diagrams of sexual intercourse and details of sexual organs during intercourse, in hand-drawings.

Momose Takato 百瀬隆人. *Me de miru sei seikatsu* 目で見る性生活. Yūki shobō, Tokyo, 1968(?) ; illustrated.
A work illustrating positions in intercourse and explaining techniques for husband and wife to practice. Some juxtaposed diagrams.

Natsukawa Bunshō 夏川文章, " *Yojōhan fusuma no shitabari* " 四畳半襖の下張, KK, 10/64, 173–201.
Research on a famous fictional work by Nagai Kafū 永井荷風, the publication of which led to a criminal indictment. The writer narrates the circumstances of publication, critically compares editions of this erotic fictional work, and concludes from the evidence that Nagai Kafū was its author.
The term *Yojōhan*, meaning a 4–1/2 mat room, got its amorous connotations from someone once having discovered erotic writings on the sliding doors of a room that size. In modern usage, it refers to covert dalliance.

Ono Jōtoku 小野常徳. *Me de miru sei seikatsu nyūmon* 眼でみる性生活入門. Amatoriasha あまとりあ社, Tokyo, March, 1968 (27th printing).
Diagrams of sex organs ; considerable textual explanations. There is much more information in this work than in most of the Japanese " technique books " of this kind. This is a very popular type of book at present (October, 1968) and but one of many. A bookstore in Tokyo Station (the Yaesu side) called *Eishōbō* 榮松房 specializes in selling these works.

Sugi Yasusaburō, Ph.d. 杉靖三郎, and 4 other Ph.d.s. *Shashin de miru sei*

seikatsu no tekunikku 写真で見る性生活のテクニック Yūki shobō, Tokyo, July, 1968; illustrated.
Woman shown alone in a variety of positions, from pre-play to orgasm, supported by detailed explanatory Japanese text. Some diagrams with male-female juxtaposed, but unclear.

Takahashi Tetsu 高橋鐵. *Seiten kenkyū* 性典研究. Tokyo, 1946.
Professor Takahashi cites this sexological study in his introduction to the pre-Meiji (1834) classic on sex, *Shikidō kimpishō* (q.v.). He gives outlines in this work of various Japanese sexological classics.

" *Takahashi Tetsu shi tai fukanshō josei gonin* " 高橋鐵氏対不感症女性五人, in Josei jishin 女性自身, Tokyo, August 26, 1968, 140–43.
The record of a special meeting held between sexologist Takahashi Tetsu and five Japanese housewives who were suffering from frigidity. A movie on aspects of sexuality was shown, after which the sexologist questioned each wife in turn about her specific problems.

Tatsuoka, Robert T., and Kozuka Sen, tr. Dr. Sha Kokken. *A Happier Sex Life*. Ikeda Shoten, Tokyo, 1967; illustrated, index.
The English translation of a Taiwanese doctor's self-advertised " study in modern Japanese sexual habits." Wooden dolls are used to illustrate positions of intercourse, and information is provided on various sexual aspects. This is the type of general sex guidebook common in the West rather than something specifically " oriental." Japanese sexological texts are not mentioned.

Usui Tsunao 臼井綱夫. *Me de miru sei seikatsu sanbyaku-roku-ju-go nichi* 眼で見る性生活三六五日. Amatoriasha, Tokyo, 1968.
Claims to teach year-round love techniques through showing hundreds of illustrations; not personally seen.

General Index